On The Home Front

Barking and Dagenham in World War II

Compiled by
Tony Clifford, Kathryn Abnett and Peter Grisby

BARKING & DAGENHAM
LIBRARIES DEPARTMENT
1990

© LONDON BOROUGH OF BARKING AND DAGENHAM

ISBN 0 900325 10 0

PRINTED IN ENGLAND BY B & S DAVIES PRINTING COMPANY 04027 23544/23011

Foreword

Thank you for your letter regarding the book you are publishing about life in your Borough during the Second World War.

As a lad of 17 I had joined the R.A.F., it was 1940 and after training at Weston-super-Mare, I was posted to the aerodrome at Hornchurch.

The Battle of Britain, as it came to be called, was at its height, the Luftwaffe made their flight paths up the River Thames past Dagenham – past Barking and eventually to London's East End.

I was a small cog in the large wheel that endeavoured to keep the Spitfires flying, but during off duty moments my pals and self would find our way to the local pubs – there were quite a few, the Harrow at Barking, the Merry Fiddlers at Becontree Heath, the Round House and several others, the ones we flocked to were the pubs that provided music.

I could sing a song or two and would be singled out by the compère to give out with songs like "If I had my way" and "Apple Blossom Time".

It was during this time I met my lovely wife Blossom, a W.A.A.F. whose home was at Rush Green, Romford. We married both at nineteen and when peace came, my area in London had been bombed badly so we thankfully took a small house in Rush Green, Dagenham. We stayed for a couple of years and I got to know the area fairly well.

As a semi pro, I took engagements at many British Legion clubs and what were known as Working Men's Clubs around the Barking, East Ham and Dagenham areas.

I was sometimes paid five guineas for the night, which sounded a lot, but when you think I used to work a fifty-four hour week as a carpenter for almost the same amount.

It didn't take me long to figure out which road to take. So, as I tell my audience " . . . although the war was very sad for some, I came out on the plus side – I got a wife, a career and a new suit – nowadays I still have the same wife – my career is still doing well and Patrick Moore is still wearing the suit!"

I wish you much success with your publication.
Warm regards,
Yours sincerely, *Max Bygraves*

I am pleased to have been asked to provide a foreword to this book which shows various aspects of what life was like for the rescue services and public alike on the home front in Barking and Dagenham during the Second World War.

Even after half a century, my adventure with an enormous magnetic mine in the River Roding at Barking is still one of my most vivid, treasured memories. Without the instant and gallant co-operation of all concerned in the surroundings, Tuckwell and I could not even have started to tackle it.

Lieutenant Commander John Duppa-Miller, GC

Introduction

In 1939, the Becontree housing estate was described as the largest municipal housing estate in the world. The German aerial photograph reproduced in this book shows how the whole of the area was a sitting target during enemy bombing attacks directed at industry and docks on the Thames. Fortunately, many of the bombs dropped on open spaces such as marshes, parks and Hainault Forest. Industrial production was – remarkably – affected very little through war damage, one important exception being the Gas Light & Coke Company's works at Beckton, which was seriously damaged on 7th September 1940, when the first large air raid was launched on London by enemy bombers.

However, many bombs did find a target, and the consequences are recorded in the pictures and statistics in this book. In a book of this size we cannot hope to give a comprehensive listing of all bombing incidents. The pictures used show the devastation which occurred when a bomb of whatever type made contact with an inhabited area or exploded before impact. We have been unable to locate or date precisely some of the photographs of bomb damage.

This is not an exhaustive history of Barking and Dagenham during the Second World War. We have attempted to show in scrapbook form the effects of the War on the populations of Barking and Dagenham, faced with terrible air raids, evacuation of families, and the loss of homes, relatives and friends. We show some of the people who were busy defending the home front and operating rescue services – for example, the Home Guard, ARP wardens, police, fire and ambulance services, and Women's Voluntary Service. The text is illustrated with accounts written by local people, taken from published and unpublished sources. We have used illustrations of local people and local scenes. Our main limitation has been selecting from the relatively small number of local photographs available. Unless otherwise acknowledged, illustrations, newspaper cuttings and reminiscences are taken from the local history collections at Valence Library and Valence House Museum. The statistics reproduced speak for themselves. Whenever possible we have tried to obtain permission to use copyright or original material.

The involvement of local firms in the war effort was tremendous, as was the contribution made in Barking and Dagenham to the various National Savings schemes.

The history of Dagenham during World War II has been recorded in *Danger over Dagenham*, published by the Borough Council in 1947. This contains a wealth of information about all aspects of the war effort on the home front, and includes a roll of honour of those killed by enemy action. Also recommended is *Ford at war*, which gives much information about the tremendous industrial production at the Dagenham factory during this period. Unfortunately, no such account for Barking exists, but we are fortunate in having had access to scrapbooks of newspaper cuttings compiled by various Departments of Barking Borough Council and by the late Colonel E.A. Loftus. Other items for further reading and study are listed in the bibliography.

In compiling this book, we are particularly grateful for help received from: Mr George Robery; Rhône-Poulenc (UK) Ltd (May & Baker); Corporate History Office, Ford Motor Company, Brentwood; Valence House Museum; Battle of Britain Prints International; Barking & Dagenham Post; Mr Norman Baker; Mrs Ruby Dymond; Mr Wally Blanchard; Miss Phyllis Pugh.

Dedication

We dedicate this book to those residents of the former Boroughs of Barking and Dagenham who made the supreme sacrifice during the World War, 1939-1945, either whilst serving with His Majesty's forces or as a result of enemy air attack.

The Barking Book of Remembrance can be viewed in the Central Reference Library, Barking; the one for Dagenham may be seen at the Civic Centre, Dagenham.

Barking Branch of the Old Contemptibles, taken at the Capitol Cinema, East St., Barking, 1937. They held meetings in the Drill Hall, Queens Road, Barking.

Aerial View of the Civic Centre, 1938. Built in 1937, the basement of the Civic Centre acted as a control room and report centre for Dagenham during the Second World War.

The Dagenham Post

BARKING AND RAINHAM GUARDIAN

NO. 1890 | Local Office: 242, HEATHWAY, DAGENHAM. Chief Office: 34, HIGH RD., ILFORD. | FRIDAY, SEPTEMBER 8, 1939 | TELEPHONES: RAINHAM 2850. ILFORD 2543. | ONE PENNY

DAGENHAM'S WAR COMMITTEE OF THREE

DAGENHAM'S WAR-TIME BIG THREE ARE:

The Mayor, Alderman A. F. J. Chorley.

Alderman R. J. D. Clack, chairman of the A.R.P. Committee.

Councillor F. Brown, chairman of the Fire Brigade Committee.

These three members of the local authority constitute the Emergency Committee which has powers to make any urgent decision.

Ordinary Committee and Council meetings have been suspended.

"War Cabinet."

The Emergency Committee in fact becomes the local authority and together with certain officials forms the Borough's "War Cabinet." They have complete civil defence authority.

The war-time officers are as follows:

Mr. F. C. Lloyd (Borough Surveyor and Engineer), Controlling Officer for A.R.P. and A.F.S.

Mr. H. O. Bigg (Treasurer), Food Controller.

Mr. J. G. O'Leary (Librarian), Fuel Controller.

Mr. G. Evans Jones (Deputy Town Clerk), National Registration Officer.

Dr. Herrington (Medical Officer of Health) takes charge of first-aid, stretcher parties, ambulances, etc.

Nearly 17,000 Evacuated From Dagenham

CHILDREN OF SCHOOL AGE, MOTHERS WITH CHILDREN UNDER SCHOOL AGE AND CERTAIN EXPECTANT MOTHERS WERE EVACUATED FROM DAGENHAM LAST FRIDAY AND SATURDAY.

They were taken from the Ford Motor Company's jetty by steamer to Yarmouth, Felixstowe and Lowestoft and then transferred to inland towns and villages.

Evacuation Figures.

The following figures show the number of persons registered for evacuation:—

School children	7,248
Non-school parties, adults	2,294
" " " Children	4,633
Expectant mothers	290
Teachers	666
Helpers	2[illegible]
Late registration of school children and mothers and children under 5	1,587
Total	16,984

A statement from the Civic Centre says:

"The Council wish to tender to everyone who assisted in the successful accomplishment of this tremendous task, performed at such short notice, their deep appreciation of the public-spirited assistance which they rendered, and to pay a tribute to the calmness and courage with which the mothers and children faced the difficulties of embarkation."

Telegrams have been received from evacuees and persons in charge of parties stating that they are all safe, comfortable and happy.

Information Bureau Opened

An information bureau is to be set up at the Civic Centre.

All inquiries should be made at this bureau no one should attempt to get into direct contact with heads of departments.

Essential Inquiries.

Local officials have a vast amount of work to cope with and only essential inquiries should be made.

MOTHER FOUND DRUNK

At Stratford Police Court on Saturday, Mrs. Winifred Hill, aged 34, of 63, Sandyhill-road, Ilford, pleaded guilty to being drunk and incapable the previous night.

P.c. Thompson said he found Mrs. Hill on the pavement and unable to take care of herself so he was forced to arrest her.

Asked if she had anything to say, Mrs. Hill said her children had all been evacuated that day and she was upset and went out to get a drink.

The Clerk (Mr. W. H. Doody): Do you consider the evacuation of your children sufficient excuse to get drunk?

The Chairman (Mr. Brodie): The Bench think it is a satisfactory excuse and you will be discharged. You have our sympathy, but try your best.

TRADESMAN'S DAUGHTER WEDS

Miss Evelyn Florence Broadway, only daughter of Mr. and Mrs. F. A. Broadway, of Crown-street, Dagenham, the well-known Old Village butchers, was married on Saturday to Mr. Patrick Horgan, son of Mr. Dennis Horgan, of Cork City, Ireland, and the late Mrs. Horgan.

The ceremony was performed by the Rev. Father Hayes, at St. Peter's Roman Catholic Church.

The bride was given away by her father. She was dressed in white floral satin with veil and orange blossom head-dress. She carried a bouquet of red carnations.

Bridesmaids were Miss G. Ellis and Miss V. Ellis, friends of the bride. One was dressed in lemon flowered satin and the other in green. Both carried bouquets of lemon carnations.

The bride's mother was dressed in navy blue georgette with hat to match.

Mr. John Downey, a friend of the groom, was best man.

After a reception at the bride's home the couple left for an unknown destination for their honeymoon.

THE HEATHWAY SERENADERS

The Dagenham Banjo, Accordion, Mandolin and Guitar Club, otherwise the Heathway Serenaders, who commence their fifth year of musical activity, include in all their concerts the plantation songs of Stephen Collins Foster.

The Club Secretary has, this week, received from the Curator of the Foster Hall Collection, University of Pittsburgh, U.S.A., a score of "Melodies of Stephen Foster," arranged for concert band by Luis Guzman, of the United States Marine Band. This is a welcome addition to the Club's library of American music.

AIR-RAID WARNING: GOOD RESPONSE

Dagenham responded well when the air-raid warning sirens were sounded last week-end.

Aroused from their beds in the early hours of Monday morning, people were soon under cover with their gas masks.

The whole district was well blacked out, but householders are warned that even a chink of light at the edge of a curtain is visible from the sky. stated.

The Heathway Serenaders. Story on this page.

Alleged Offence Under Lighting Regulations

BARKINGSIDE LICENSEE ARRESTED COURT STORY

The first case to be brought before the Stratford magistrates under the new Lighting regulations made last week, was partly heard on Tuesday, when a Barkingside licensee was remanded on bail for fourteen days, charged with a breach of the regulations.

Frederick William Boyden, 52, joint licensee and manager of the Old Maypole Hotel, Barkingside, Essex, was charged with being the person in charge of the hotel, during the hours of darkness, he caused or permitted the internal lighting inside the premises to be displayed without being so obscured as to prevent the illumination therefrom being visible from the outside, contrary to the Defence regulations Lighting Restriction Order 1939.

There was a second charge of obstructing a police officer.

Boyden pleaded not guilty to each charge.

P.c. Wakeman said at 9.55 on Monday night, in consequence of a telephone message, he went to the Old Maypole Hotel in Fencepiece-road, Barkingside, and saw that the whole of the ground floor lights in the front of the building were very poorly obscured. The windows were pasted over with a light brown paper which was far from being efficient. The fanlights over most of the windows were open. No provision had been made to obscure the lights from the openings of the fanlights, and they were showing a direct ray. The doors were glazed, and covered with a light brown paper.

There was no protection to prevent the light escaping when the doors were open and every time a door was opened there was a ray of light straight across the forecourt. He entered the public house and found it was full of customers. On his direction a member of the staff extinguished the whole of the lights after being away from the bar for about half a minute.

Witness then asked to see a responsible person on the forecourt and the defendant came out and strongly resented the action witness had taken.

The Clerk: What did he say?

P.c. Wakeman: He said "Why did you have those lights put out in my house. There was no need for it." I pointed out to him the danger, and the offence under the Defence Act, but he still continued to argue and to resent my action. I asked him for his name and address, and he said, "You have my name and address at the station." I pointed out to him that I did not know his name and address and again asked him to give it to me. He again refused, and I then said I should arrest him for failing to obscure his lights and for obstructing me in the execution of my duty. I took him to Barkingside police station where he was charged, and after the charge had been read over to him he insisted upon making a statement and having it taken down in writing.

Alleged Statement.

A statement was handed to the Clerk and he read it.

In it Boyden said that his man came to him and said that the police had just come in and ordered all the lights to be put out. "This, although it jeopardised my till, was immediately done," said the statement. I was then told the police officer wished to speak to me. I went out on to the forecourt and asked him the reason for his action and told him I had been discussing the lighting of the house with an officer sent specially from Barkingside police station. I proceeded to tell the officer about this but he would not listen to me, but threatened me with penalties. I asked him for his number which he refused to give me and when I struck a match to see it on his collar he blew the match out.

"Grasped His Arm."

"He then said 'Now I will have your name and address,' and I told him my name and address was already known to the police. He said, 'That has nothing to do with me, are you withholding your name and address?' My answer was that I could not withhold something which was known to the police. He then said 'Come on, you are under arrest,' and grasped me by the arm and marched me all the way to the police station. I reached the police station at 10.12, but was not charged until 11.15. I wish to protest against the truculent manner of the officer concerned and the manner in which the charge was brought."

From the dock, Boyden said he would not ask questions, but would like an adjournment for a fortnight so that he could be legally represented.

The Clerk said in view of the statements in the statement made by Boyden he thought it would be better if the police were legally represented as it was a serious charge liable to heavy punishment.

The case was then remanded for fourteen days, Boyden being allowed bail in his own surety of £25.

A.R.P. RECRUITS WANTED

While the Dagenham A.R.P. services are efficiently organised and ready for action, there is still need for further recruits.

Wardens and first-aid personnel are needed, also volunteers for other sections of the service.

Recruits have been coming in rapidly throughout the week and many have been enrolled at a loud-speaker van which has been touring the district broadcasting information.

SHOP ASSISTANTS UNION IN WAR TIME

The main administration of the National Amalgamated Union of Shop Assistants, Warehousemen and Clerks has been devolved from the Central Offices on to twenty War Time Administrative Offices in various parts of the country and most of the business which the branches have in the past transacted with the Central Offices will now be transacted with the appropriate War Time Administrative Office.

The following departments will continue to operate from Dilke House: Organising, Negotiations, Research, Legal and Finance.

The editorial offices of the Distributive Trades Journal will also continue at Dilke House.

MOTOR CYCLIST INJURED

Injuries to the right hand and left leg were sustained by Charles Clayton, a motor cyclist, of Goresbrook-road, Dagenham, when he came into collision with a motor lorry at the junction of Church Elm-lane and Glebe-road on Monday. The lorry driver was Mr. E. B. Clarke, of Royal Parade, Church-street, Dagenham.

EVACUEES: NEWS FROM AREAS

We have received letters from mothers in the reception areas and from persons in charge of the children, and they speak in terms of high praise of the arrangements.

Dagenham mothers at Gorleston-on-Sea, have addressed the following letter to the mothers of Dagenham:—

"We mothers who have accompanied the children would like you to know that all the children are very happy and well cared for. At the present moment they are all paddling and making sand castles on a beautiful beach. The teachers are doing all they can to make the children forget they are away from home.

"We had a wonderful welcome and everybody is showering attentions on us."

H. M. Robinson writes from Manningtree (Essex):

"I am here in charge of a detachment of Dagenham children, and I am telling the plain, honest truth when I say that they are having the time of their lives.

"The local people are doing their duty and providing board and lodging. They are also going far beyond their mere duty, and are making clothes, buying shoes and doing all they can for those who are ill provided.

"The children are blackberrying, swimming, and revelling in the, to them, novel life of the village.

"We are in constant touch with them, going for walks, bathing with them, visiting them in their billets. We see them sitting down to generous meals, and hear of nothing but kindness, while from 'uncles,' 'aunties,' 'grandads' and 'grannies' we hear excellent reports of the behaviour of the children.

"Of course, there were trying moments on the journey and a few tears from over-tired children who were also perhaps hungry, and certainly upset by the strangeness of everything. But Dagenham mothers need have no anxiety about their evacuated children. As one little girl said to her brother when she heard that there were kittens, a dog, and chickens to be fed, 'We've clicked, mate.'"

WEDDING OF LOCAL INTEREST

A wedding of considerable local interest took place at Dagenham Parish Church on Saturday, when Mr. Donald Eric West, youngest son of Mr. and Mrs. Edward J. West, of The White House, Dagenham, was married to Miss Grace Evelyn Barton, only daughter of Mr. and Mrs. William C. Barton, of 91, Fanshawe-crescent, Dagenham.

The bridegroom's parents are very well known in the district, particularly in the Old Village. Mr. West has been connected with the Parish Church for many years, and served for a considerable period as churchwarden. He was also a member of the old Parish Council and has taken an active interest in several forms of social work. Mr. West is a member of the firm of West and Coe, the undertakers.

Rev. A. MacKinnon, Vicar of Beeby, Leicester, a former curate at the Parish Church, performed the ceremony, assisted by Rev. T. W. House, the present senior curate.

The bride, who was given away by her father, wore a gown of white lace, with a panel inset of white satin frills. She carried a sheaf of white arum lilies, and wore a string of pearls, the gift of the bridegroom.

The bridesmaids were Miss A. Bickle and Miss Melba Walmsley, friends of the bride. Miss Barbara Kemp and Miss Lesley Hill acted as train-bearers.

Mr. Jack West, brother of the bridegroom, acted as best man, and the service was choral. Mr. G. J. Andrews was the organist. The church was decorated with gladioli.

The reception was held at the Methodist Church, Rainham-road South, and the honeymoon was spent at Newquay, Cornwall.

EVACUATION: COUNCIL'S VISIT

News has been received that parties under the evacuation scheme have entered their final billets in villages in Norfolk and Suffolk.

Dagenham Council despatched a small committee yesterday to inspect billets and se...

Cyclist Killed Under Bus At Broadway

LIFTING GEAR FROM POLICE STATION

THE FIRST FATAL ACCIDENT IN A BLACK-OUT SINCE THE CRISIS OCCURRED IN ILFORD ON FRIDAY NIGHT.

A pedal cyclist, Mr. Harold Arthur Tremble, aged 41, of 14, Mascalle-lane, Brentwood, was run over by a London Transport motor 'bus at Station Approach, Ilford Broadway, just after 10 p.m.

At the inquest, held at the Town Hall on Tuesday, it was disclosed that the wife of the deceased was shortly expecting a child and for that reason was unable to attend the inquiry.

The Coroner, Dr. P. B. Skeels, sat with a jury who recorded a verdict of "Accidental Death," exonerating the driver of the 'bus from all blame.

Evidence of identification was given by Mrs. Ida Mary Oliver, of Mascalle-lane, Brentwood.

A plan of the scene of the accident was produced by P.c. Norman Smith, stationed at Ilford. Witness added that deceased was travelling towards Barkingside from Station-approach when the accident occurred.

Medical evidence was given by Dr. John Erskine Malcom, who said that Mr. Tremble was admitted on Friday night to King George Hospital between 10 and 11 p.m. He was dead when admitted. Every rib of his body was broken on both sides and the pelvis was crushed. These extensive injuries were consistent with having been run over by the wheels of a heavy vehicle.

Death was due to shock and the multiple injuries.

A.R.P. Warden's Evidence.

Mr. Ernest Leslie Milton, an A.R.P. warden, of 5, Uphall-avenue, Ilford, said that he was walking near the Station-approach at the time of the accident.

"I was standing at the corner of Cranbrook-road and the High-road looking down Ilford Hill, and the first I knew of the accident was when I saw an approaching 'bus lift on its front near-side," he added. "It seemed to lift again at the back and at the same time there was a slight crash.

"I thought at the time it was an accident and I ran across. All I could see were the remains of a bike in the middle of the road, and I didn't think then that anyone had been hurt.

"The 'bus continued, very slowly, and I ran after it and shouted to the 'bus to stop. The conductor flashed a light under the 'bus and we found a man underneath at the back of the vehicle."

Answering the Coroner, witness said that it was a very dangerous night for any cyclist to be out. He agreed that the 'bus was travelling very slowly and was completely under control.

Witness added that he did not see the cyclist before the accident occurred.

'Bus Stopped.

The conductor of the 'bus, Mr. John Mancey, said that the 'bus stopped at the traffic lights at the cross roads in Ilford High-road. As the 'bus pulled away again he felt a bump and he thought that one of the back wheels of the 'bus had hit the nearside kerb.

"I then heard someone shouting 'Stop, stop,'" continued witness, "and I rang the emergency bell and the 'bus stopped at once. I walked round the near side and I saw a man's head protruding from between the life-guard. He was quite a yard from the first pair of back wheels.

"After we stopped I saw a pedal cycle about two yards behind the 'bus."

Lifting gear was obtained from the Ilford Police Station and the man was extracted.

The driver of the 'bus, Mr. Henry Albert Webb, said that he was in the act of changing into second gear, when he heard the emergency bell ring. He did not see a bicycle and was surprised when he discovered that the 'bus had just run over a cyclist.

With regard to the bump, witness said that he thought this was due to the fact that he had misjudged his distance in the dark and that the back nearside wheels had mounted the kerb.

Witness added that he had been driving for 25 years on the same route, and he had been awarded twelve Safety First certificates.

At the time of the accident he was eight minutes behind schedule. He was also driving with his wind-screen wide open in order to improve his vision.

Bicycle Damaged.

P.c. Ernest Handscomb, stationed at Ilford, said that the injured man was under the nearside of the 'bus between the front and the back wheel. The bicycle was badly damaged.

Without retiring the jury returned the verdict already stated.

COUNCIL SERVICE TEMPORARILY SUSPENDED

Normal public services in Dagenham, such as refuse collection and street sweeping, have been partially suspended for the time being.

The local authority ask residents for "co-operation and no complaints" on this score.

ALL SCHOOLS CLOSED

All schools in Dagenham are closed until further notice.

Evacuated children will attend schools in various reception areas.

Children remaining in the town will not have to attend classes.

Dagenham prepares for war.

YOUR BLACK-OUT

Test your black-out room by room. When it is really dark, view your windows from the bottom of the garden or the other side of the street.

There is no excuse for bad black-out. In halls, passages, lavatories, and on landings where bright, white light is not essential, use blue or other tinted lamps of low wattage. A bedside light to undress by need be little more than a glimmer. In your living rooms, however, have the same light as in peace time. Plenty of light makes for cheerfulness.

Here are some things you can do to improve the black-out in any room where it is not yet perfect:

(1) Shade your lights so that the light is not on the windows.
(2) Line existing curtains with suitable material.
(3) Provide a blind to cover the whole of the window space, with, if possible, six inches overlap on either side and at the bottom.
(4) Tack curtains at the side, so that they do not creep along and let the light in.
(5) Provide the inner edges of the curtains with small safety pins, so that when drawn they can be fastened and prevent gaping.
(6) Across a bay window, fix draw curtains of suitable material, so that the bay is cut off from the rest of the room after black-out. The bay windows must, of course, have their ordinary curtains drawn. If properly carried out, this provides a perfect black-out.
(7) Cut strips of black-out paper 5-6 inches wide, and paste firmly down the sides and top and bottom of windows where light filters through.

Properly planned and made black-out arrangements do *not* interfere with ventilation.

Black-out advice from Dagenham's official handbook.

HEATHWAY REPERTORY COMPANY
Production of "The farmer's wife",
Saturday, December 9th, 1939.

HEATHWAY REPERTORY COMPANY.

SUCCESSFUL BLACK-OUT PRODUCTION.

A few weeks ago it seemed as though amateur dramatics would be among the first war "casualties," but there are already signs that it takes more than a black-out to extinguish our enthusiastic players. The Heathway Repertory Company is among those who have decided to go ahead as usual, and their enterprise was splendidly supported at their first war-time production on Saturday night. This was Eden Phillpotts' famous play, "The Farmer's Wife," given at the Osborn Hall, Heathway, and advertised in advance as "a glorious black-out relief." The crowded audience who braved the darkness obviously agreed with the description, and their enthusiasm as well as their numbers was a tribute to the Society.

As usual, the play was produced by Miss Beatrice R. Holley, with back-stage assistance from Mr. Charles Rose (stage manager), Mr. Stanley Hooker, his assistant, Mr. Peter Legon (stage carpenter) and Mr. George North (electrician). "The Farmer's Wife," though always sure of a welcome, is not an easy production for amateurs, for the long cast is likely to seem unwieldy on a small or average stage. The difficult second act was extremely well handled on Saturday, from this point of view, for the grouping had evidently been well planned. The players were particularly level in standard, Mr. Arthur E. Gee making admirable capital of his opportunities as the Farmer. He had just the right suggestion of pomposity and self-esteem, spoke extremely well, and never allowed the comedy to run ahead into exaggeration. His punctured conceit after being rejected in matrimony was always amusingly shown, and this acting had genuine quality. Both of the daughters were effective, Miss Betty Bleach being suitably vivacious and casual as "Petronell," while Miss Barbara Shaw allowed "Sibley" to be a little too shadowy throughout. There is not a great deal of scope in this part, but the...

The Heathway Repertory Company

President: Vice-President:
Mr. JOHN PARKER, M.P.   Mrs. PROSSER-EVANS.

present

"The Farmer's Wife"

(by Eden Phillpotts)

ACTS I. and III take place at Applegarth Farm.
ACT II. at the Villa Residence of Miss Thirza Tapper.

5 minutes interval between Acts I & II.
15 minutes interval between Acts II & III

Cast.

Samuel Sweetland	... ...	ARTHUR E. GEE
Petronell Sweetland	... ...	BETTY BLEACH
Sibley Sweetland	... ...	BARBARA SHAW
Araminta Dench	... ...	RITA GARDNER
Churdles Ash	... ...	FREDERICK HOLE
Old Henry Coaker	... ...	RONALD TARBARD
Richard Coaker	... ...	STANLEY HOOKER
Mrs. Smerdon	... ...	PEGGY BARKER
George Smerdon	... ...	REGINALD BARKER
Sophie Smerdon	... ...	MAUREEN JONES
Teddy Smerdon	... ...	EMANUEL SCHNEIDER
Thirza Tapper	... ...	BEATRICE R. HOLLEY
Mary Hearn	... ...	JOAN DAY
Louisa Windeatt	... ...	JOAN CALVER
Valiant Dunnybrig	... ...	CHARLES ROSE
Susan Maine	... ...	VIOLET DOWELL
The Rev. Septimus Tudor	...	ARCHIBALD PHILLIPS
Hon. Mrs. Tudor	... ...	GEORGE E. MOORE
Doctor Rundle	... ...	ARTHUR KEMP
Mrs. Rundle	... ...	OLIVE BATEMAN
Mr. Gregson	... ...	

The Plymouth Glee Singers :—

MARGARET ANGUS
OLIVE BATEMAN
HILDA FREEMAN
GEORGE NORTH
GEORGE ANGUS

The play produced by   BEATRICE R. HOLLEY

The Company is being assisted on this occasion by The Dagenham Orchestra who are playing the entr'acte music
Conductor - Alfred Jones, A.R.C.M.

Stage Manager	Charles Rose
Assistant Stage Manager ...	Stanley Hooker
Stage Carpenter	Peter Legon
Lighting by	George North

Red Curtains used in Act II. from the Stage Box of the Gaiety Theatre, London.

Secretary ... ... Frederick Dowell
1100, Green Lane, Dagenham.

A Representative of the "Grays & Tilbury Gazette" will be present during the evening.

Ration Book issued to Mrs. Ellen Boreham, who was a diabetic, hence the sugar ration has been removed.

Norman and Doris Baker.

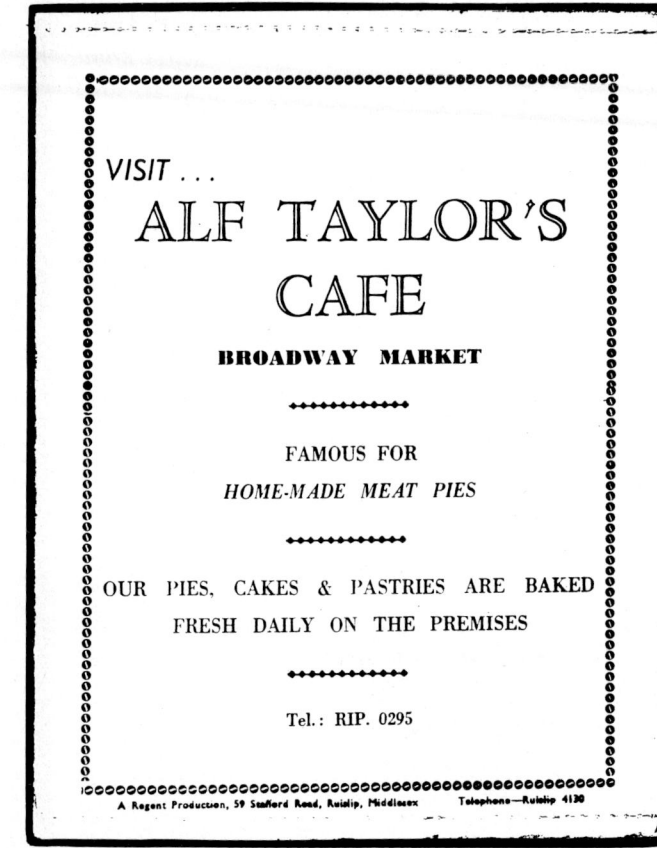

VISIT...

ALF TAYLOR'S CAFE

BROADWAY MARKET

FAMOUS FOR
HOME-MADE MEAT PIES

OUR PIES, CAKES & PASTRIES ARE BAKED
FRESH DAILY ON THE PREMISES

Tel.: RIP. 0295

RATION BOOK HOLDER

FARMER'S MEAT STORES

Family Butchers

COOKED MEATS AND
SAUSAGES OUR SPECIALITY

EAST STREET, BARKING
Telephone: RIPpleway 2352

130a MORLEY ROAD
BROADWAY MARKET
BARKING
Telephone: RIPpleway 0141

Rationing

The rationing system was born in 1938 in order to ensure the equitable feeding of the entire population. The first ration books were issued in January, 1940. At the beginning only meat was rationed, but, shortly after, margarine, butter, fats, bacon, sugar, tea, etc., could only be obtained by means of the ration book. Later on, as commodities became difficult to obtain, the "points" system was put into operation.

Norman Baker, of Maybury Road, Thames View, still has his ration book and associated items in a scrap book, as our photograph shows. We are grateful to the Barking and Dagenham Post for the photograph and the following account of Mr Baker's war years:

"The Blitz years are remembered with fear and concern by Norman Baker, but they have been treasured ever since, and he still has his ration book and ID card to prove it.

During the War, Norman lived in Ripple Road, Barking.

"I remember late one evening there was a knock at the door and we found some foreign civilians huddled together in some rubble. Thinking they were Germans we took them to the police, only to find they were Norwegian sailors, gone AWOL", says Norman.

Norman was forced to work in an essential industry during the War because the Armed Forces Act made him ineligible for service. He worked in Southern United Telephone Cables at Dagenham Dock.

"I was returning from a wedding with my two sister-in-laws when a bomb blast knocked us across the road. We'd just been missed by a land mine dropped by parachute", Norman remembered.

"When the Germans sent the Doodle Bugs over the first one was sent with a plane which was shot down by the big guns in spare ground by the Docks. My step-father managed to retrieve the German's helmet and insignia as mementoes".

"I treasure all those memories", Norman told us. "We've kept all our ration books, ID cards, tax papers and clothing coupons – they were hard days. We had to work at least 56 hours a week and help with fire watching".

Despite the horrors of war, Norman still remembers them happily as the years he and Doris courted. "She means more to me than a pot of gold", he fondly remembers of the lady who got him through the war".

Some of the children, with their teachers, evacuated from Dagenham to Norfolk, making the best of things at a Christmas party in a Colby school.

16,984 registered for evacuation in Dagenham:

School children (with 666 teachers
 and 266 helpers) 7,248
Mothers and children 8,514
Expectant mothers 290

J. G. O'Leary, compiler of "Danger over Dagenham", allows himself a moment of emotion in his official account:

"One personal impression – an awful silence. The children did not sing".

Using ships provided by the General Steam Navigation Company, the evacuation of Dagenham children took place from the Ford Motor Company loading jetties on Friday, 1st September and Saturday, 2nd September, 1939.

Evacuees from Gascoigne Road School, Barking.

The following accounts were written by evacuees from St Margaret's Church of England School, Barking, and were printed in their school magazine for Christmas 1944.

Where I was evacuated to, Clitheroe, I had a music teacher and she used to teach children to play the piano and 'cello. We went into the fields and watched the sheep and cows. We sometimes saw the cows milked by an Italian prisoner, who told us that he had been captured when he was nineteen, and said he did not like Hitler or Mussolini.

Jean Rudge.

At Welwyn stands the Shredded Wheat factory. There are about 200 people working there. Outside the town most of the people live in thatched cottages surrounded by fields in which corn and crops are grown. Near by there is a dairy farm where over sixty Jersey and other breeds of cows are kept. Every day these cows are milked by machinery.

John Debenham.

I was evacuated to a place in Stoke-on-Trent called Meir. I was in a greengrocer's house, and I had apples and all kinds of fruit. In Stoke-on-Trent I did not like it because it was too smoky. I had some friends down there, but they are not like my friends at home.

John Sibley.

The place I went to was in Cheshire. We were billeted in what used to be soldiers' barracks. There were farms all around us, and one day the welfare lady asked if any boy would like a job on a farm. A lot of us went and we had to do potato picking. We could reach two seaside places, one on the side of the River Dee, called Parkgate; the other was Birkenhead.

Stanley Hillden.

When I went to St. Anne's away from the fly-bombs, the streets seemed different, with all the lamps alight, and you could see the sea, because you only had to go across the road and walk across the sands and you were there.

G. White.

The first day we got down there in Kent, three doodlebugs came over but did no harm. We went plum picking, and a few days before we came home I had a ride on my dad's horse.

Joan Murphy.

I was evacuated to a small town called Maryport. It has a dock, and boats come in from Ireland for coal. I went to Keswick, it is all hills and lakes, and you see men in boats fishing. You also can see islands in the middle of the lakes. Maryport is pretty, when the fishermen come in and when they go out to sea. Maryport has a population of 10,000 people, and the Member of Parliament is Mr. Cap.

R. Storey.

I did not go, because if I went I should want to come home again, so I might as well stay at home.

Joan Hart.

I was very lucky indeed, I went to a nice clean billet in Burnley, Lancashire, with a lady called Mrs. Lowe. She was very kind to me. Burnley is a cotton town dotted with tall chimneys and mills. The lady worked what they call a six loom in Nelson's mill.

Mary Rickett.

When I went to Northampton, I played up in the tree where there were lots of apples. I went into the woods and I saw a rabbit run into a hole. I had a look into the hole and a lump of clay went in my eye and made it keep on watering.

Ivan St. Pier.

When I went to Furnex Pelem, I lived with my Nan. They have no gas or electricity so they have oil lamps.

Mrs Ruby Dymond has lived in Oglethorpe Road, Dagenham, since 1935. We are grateful to the Barking & Dagenham Post for permission to use the evacuation memories which follow.

Ruby Dymond was evacuated with her three children a couple of days before war broke out. They were billeted with an American millionairess, Mrs Myers, at her home, Erwarton Rectory, near Harwich. The youngsters had to walk two miles to get to school, next to the naval base at Shotley.

Mrs Dymond recalls that Mrs Myers had her own staff of servants. She used to take the French poodles for walks through the snow. She didn't meet a soul and the silence was intense.

Later in 1940, Mrs Myers moved and Ruby and the children went to Kenilworth in Warwickshire. "At first we were billeted with an elderly couple, but then I was asked to look after four other children while their mother was in hospital. We were given a tumbledown cottage and were later told the living room was over a well that had water in it".

While they were in Kenilworth, a landmine dropped in the High Street killing 21 people. It was very close to where Ruby was staying, and was such a frightening experience that her hair turned white.

The family were close to Coventry, which suffered badly from bombing raids and Ruby saw the terrible fires in the city caused by enemy action. She concludes: "We returned in 1942 thinking we would be just as safe at home".

Mrs Dymond's daughter Sylvia with Chloe at Erwarton Rectory, May 1940.

THE battle of Britain—the Premier's phrase yesterday — has begun. Following severe R.A.F. bombing in the Ruhr, the Rhineland and at Hamburg, German 'planes raided the Thames Estuary late last night.

A raider was shot down in East Anglia by a fighter. Watchers cheered as the bomber crashed in flames.

Searchlights and A.A. guns were in action, and a number of bombs were dropped.

Air-raid warnings were also sounded in Cambridgeshire, Suffolk, Lincolnshire, Norfolk, Northamptonshire and at an Essex town; A.A. fire was heard and R.A.F. fighters went up.

Several Nazi 'planes were caught in the searchlights in the Thames Estuary raid. Searchlights were attacked by machine-gun fire.

See also Back Page.

Let All The Children Go To Safety

THE six-day evacuation from London has ended. These boys and girls have been sent by their parents to the West Country. But about 340,000 children remain in Greater London.

Arrangements should be made at once to remove all children from crowded cities—if necessary to Canada, which has offered to shelter thousands.

France's Foreign Minister has said that his country " has merely asked Germany under what conditions she would consent to stop the slaughter of French children." We shall fight all the better if we know that the children are safe.

Evacuees from Green Lane School, 1940.

Dagenham evacuees at Yarmouth, 2nd September, 1939.

My Memories as an Evacuee 1939

by Miss Phyllis Pugh,
formerly of Parsloes Avenue, Dagenham

Well, it all started on September 1st 1939, and the memory still lingers strongly. We, meaning my sisters Elsie aged 11 years and Rosetta (Rosie for short) who was just 6 years old, gathered with other school-children outside Spurling Road School. We all carried a variety of cases, hold-alls, rucksacks containing a change of clothes, some sandwiches and, of course, our gas-masks.

From the school we walked to Dagenham Dock, accompanied by my mother, with Rosie crying incessantly as she complained of the long journey. Elsie could not have cared less, regarding it as high adventure. I was the eldest at 13 years and was deemed to be in charge and had to act the part.

On arrival at the Docks we boarded a Thames paddle steamer and we were told we were being taken to Great Yarmouth in case of war. Well, as one can imagine, it was a long and tiring journey lasting nine hours, luckily the weather was mild. On disembarking we walked to a school somewhere in the town where we were issued with a palliasse and a blanket. We had a meal of cold saveloys and lemonade against a background of Rosie crying for her mother.

On Saturday (2nd) we were taken to the beach to play and I remember two ladies buying us some rock. Lunch was the usual cold saveloys – no hot meals all the time we were there.

On Sunday 3rd we were told that war had been declared and soon after the announcement came the first air-raid warning, a fearful sound but happily a false alarm.

The next day we moved inland and were each issued with 'iron rations' – a tin of corned beef, a pound of biscuits and a half-pound bar of Cadbury's milk chocolate (and a warning that in no way were we to eat them). We then boarded buses for an unknown destination. Half way we stopped for sandwiches and a drink and here met my eldest brother's wife – Ivy and her two children Leonard and Sylvia. The girl was about 2 months old and the boy about 2 years.

We re-boarded buses and eventually arrived at our final stopping place, a village called Thorpe Market.

We were put down on the village green and then the fun began. Fun being the word for indignity. We were to be housed in private homes – the owners being allowed to choose who they wanted. How they decided I will never know, perhaps it was best dressed, best scrubbed, the right sex and the number in family. All I remember was the humiliation of the whole scene (akin to a slave or cattle market). We three were separated, Elsie being led off and Rosie and I taken to a cottage owned by a 90 year old spinster – it must have been a last-minute choice of billet.

Our landlady was very kind and gave us our first hot meal for days. We also enjoyed our first good wash. Rosie cried for mum throughout the night and, on reflection, I still wonder how mothers must have felt at parting with their children to unknown homes and places, but the fear of invasion and the first target being London, helped to strengthen their resolve.

Weston Mercury
Waterloo Street, Weston-super-Mare.
tting from issue dated......25 Dec 1943..............

BARKING ABBEY TELLS ITS WESTON STORY

ITS EVENTFUL THREE YEARS OF EVACUATION

GRACEFUL TRIBUTE TO TOWN'S HOSPITALITY

The December issue of "The Barkabbeyan," the magazine of the Barking Abbey School, is the first to be published for four years, and is of special interest to Westonians, for it is largely devoted to a chronicle of school activities from September, 1939, to July, 1942, the period during which the School was evacuated to Weston-super-Mare.

Mr. M. Wollman, in an editorial, says: "Looking back on our three years at Weston we form the conclusion that the gain outweighs the loss. We encountered a way of life and an environment very different from ours; we grew to recognise its dignity and worth. We all have memories of those three years, memories that will always linger with us. Each one of us has his own, but we all share, pre-eminently, the memory of the glories and the history of the Somerset countryside—the charm of Brean Down, the homeliness of Worlebury Woods, the awe of Cheddar Gorge, the majesty of Wells Cathedral, the benediction of Glastonbury Abbey, the wind-swept spaciousness of Blackdown.... Revivified, we returned to Barking."

A Dark, Wet Evening.

Miss D. L. Holloway, who was Acting Headmistress at Weston, pens a detailed story of the School's experiences in the town, from which we cull the following extracts:

"The school party, about 250 strong, complete with luggage, gas masks and food, departed from Upney Station (on Sept. 1st, 1939), doubtless with deep feelings of depression and foreboding behind smiling faces, feelings of deep anxiety for those left behind to face the threatened air raids and terrors. Later, spirits rose somewhat on learning that our destination was Weston-super-Mare.

We arrived at that now familiar town about 9 p.m. on a dark, wet evening, passing to our distribution centres at Grove Park and Locking-road, where we were kindly received and generously refreshed before being taken to billets. We were so late in arriving that the billets earmarked for us at the south side of the town had been taken up by mothers and children arriving on the previous train, and we found ourselves placed at the northern end of the town, with the school we were to share at the extreme south. However, changes were made when possible, and the position became easier and more satisfactory as we became better known in the town.

A Debt of Gratitude to Weston.

"We owe a debt of gratitude to the local officials and inhabitants of Weston for their kindness and help. Many were voluntary workers, who devoted all their time and energy to the comfort and well-being of the thousands of evacuated people sent to this town.

"The work of finding billets, moving the boys and girls when necessary, and dealing with many of the difficulties arising in connection with the billets, fell mainly on the helpers, who kept daily contact between the school and town authorities.

"This important work requiring so much tact and patience was done with great success by Mrs. Davies, Mrs. White and Mrs. Richardson, who was replaced later by Mrs. Driver. They were untiring in their efforts to get the pupils happily placed in homes where they felt they were wanted.

"It was an ordeal for the boy or girl to be put into a strange home in a strange town, but it was almost as great an ordeal for the foster-parent whose home was thus invaded. Both had to make adjustments and allowances, and many were the difficulties dealt with at school from pupils, parents and foster-parents.

A Friendly Co-operation.

"The pupils were divided into small groups, each in charge of a member of the staff, who visited the billet regularly and who gave help and advice to the boy or girl in difficulty. A friendly co-operation between teacher and pupil and between teacher and foster-parent was thus established, and the foster parent became interested in the school and its work.

"Next in importance to the billeting were the arrangements at school for education. We shared the local County School, at first occupying a part of both the Boys' and Girls' Schools, but later, in Oct., 1940, when Mitcham County School arrived in Weston, requiring accommodation, we transferred entirely to the Girls' School. The Headmistress, staff and girls did their utmost to make us happy and comfortable. When they were approached over any difficulty the question invariably was, "How can we help you?" It does not require much imagination to realise some of the difficulties when four schools share one building, difficulties arising from noise, breakages, cloakroom accommodation, laboratory arrangements, etc.

More Tuition Than in Normal Times !

"The County School occupied the building in the mornings, and we had our lessons in the afternoons, from 1.30 to 5.30, and on Saturday mornings from 9 to 12.30. All games and swimming lessons were taken in the mornings, in addition to some lessons taken either in the vacant rooms in the school or in a hall in the town. It is interesting to notice that the number of hours under tuition in a year well exceeded that provided under normal conditions. This was partly due to the shortened holidays and longer terms, five or six weeks being added to the usual school year. The constant changing of staff and the varying numbers of pupils made the organisation of the school difficult. . . .

Many Air Raid Warnings.

"The number of pupils had decreased from 278 to 180, partly as the result of a small enemy raid on Weston and of the frequent raid warnings. The warnings during the day became so numerous that we decided not to interrupt lessons unless our official spotter, Mr. Phillips, signalled that enemy planes were near. A number of the staff were recalled to assist with the pupils who had returned to Barking, and it became necessary to dovetail to some extent with the Mitcham County School in the matter of staffing, in order that all subjects should continue to be taught. The sixth form combined with the sixth form of Mitcham County School for some subjects, but the school always retained its own identity.

Excellent Health Services.

"The health of the pupils was carefully watched during this period of evacuation. The medical services provided by the Somerset Education Authority were excellent. Both medical and dental examinations were held each year, and treatment given where necessary. The dentist surprised some of the pupils by operating at the time of examination, so saving them the joys of anticipation. In cases of emergency, treatment was obtained through the local doctors and dentists. We had no epidemics of sickness, and the general health improved greatly from the effects of the sea breezes and outdoor exercise. . . . .

The Blitz.

"Evacuation came to a close when the Germans decided that the churches, residences and schools of Weston were military targets. On the clear moonlight nights of June 27th and 28th, 1942, the town was raided from roof-top level, and incendiary and high explosive bombs were scattered over it. On the second night showers of incendiaries caused fires in many parts of the town, and among the buildings destroyed was the County School for Girls.

"The fire spread so quickly that it was impossible to attempt to rescue anything from the west wing of the building, and all school records were burnt. The centre block and the adjoining Boys' School were saved. After each raid the staff undertook the difficult and anxious task of checking up the pupils. Those in damaged houses had been removed and had to be traced, while some had left the town with their foster-parents after the first raid and left no address. We were fortunate in finding that the only casualties from either raid were two boys, whose injuries were slight.

Exams. The Day After The Raids.

"On the day following the raids, candidates taking the Higher School Certificate and the General Schools Examination were faced with two 3-hour papers. The question papers had been burnt, so they took their examination from 12 p.m. to 3 p.m., and from 5 p.m. to 8 p.m., using the papers borrowed from Mitcham County School, after their candidates had finished.

The papers were duplicated for the following day with the kindly assistance of the Headmaster and staff of Mitcham School, and a further set arrived on Wednesday.

"Term ended on July 17th, and the boys and girls returned to Barking to the care of their parents, who had missed them sadly during their long absence.

Weston a Second Home.

"What are their thoughts and memories now of their three years in Weston? They had learnt to be self-reliant and adaptable, and to make the best of any circumstances in which they might be placed. Some had a second home in Weston and friends they could visit in future vacations. They had lived among people whose outlook was far different from that of their home surroundings in Greater London; they were in daily contact with the pupils of three other secondary schools, with whom they could exchange thoughts and opinions.

"They were fit and healthy, as the result of much time spent in walking, cycling, or playing games in the fresh air. They had learnt to appreciate the lovely scenery of the Somerset hills and to do without the attractions of the town. All these things are surely to the good, and must have some lasting influence on the character and tastes of the boy or girl.

Mind over Matter

BARKING ABBEY SCHOOL (Essex) suffered severely by enemy action. The school which it shared during evacuation at Weston-super-Mare was burned down in June 1942 and all records were lost. It returned to Barking, but last summer a flying bomb left most of the building in ruins and the school was dispersed. Despite setbacks, 20 scholarships and exhibitions were won last year.

Digging trenches for use as shelters, Vicarage Field, Barking, June 1939.

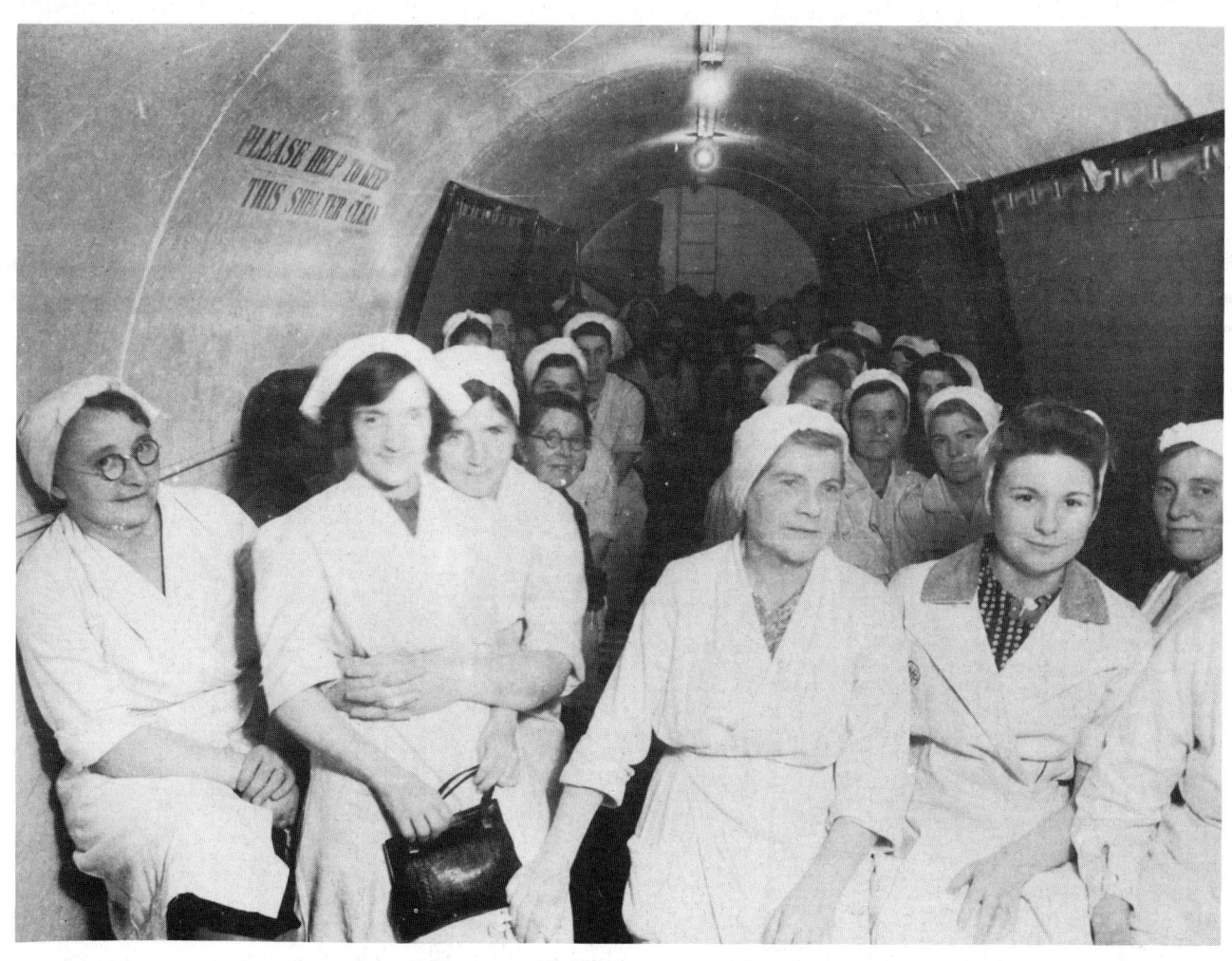

May & Baker packing girls in underground air raid shelter. The company built 31 shelters underground, plus seven on the surface and four more partly underground. (Photograph courtesy of Rhône-Poulenc (UK) Ltd.)

Vicarage Field shelters, unearthed in 1988 when building of the new shopping precinct began. These shelters were investigated by Mr A. G. Robery, who has supplied these photographs. The shelters were 200 feet long, 6 feet 6 inches high, and 5 feet 6 inches wide. The pile of soil was caused by a building lorry almost coming through the ceiling. Nothing of the shelters now remains.

Barrage balloons over Dagenham – a photograph taken from the May & Baker factory, 1943. (Photograph courtesy of Rhône-Poulenc (UK) Ltd.

RAF crew engaged in putting up barrage balloons in Barking. Photographed outside the Crooked Billet in about 1940. (Photograph courtesy of Barking and Dagenham Post).

Barking Council decontamination unit, June 1939. The personnel were part-time male volunteer workers recruited from the staff of the Borough Engineer's Department, together with operatives of certain commercial laundries in the Borough. These volunteers underwent special training to render harmless liquid poison gas. Decontamination squads were also trained in rescue work.

The following is an account of Civil Defence training by Dr. T. A. Cockburn, who was Assistant Medical Officer in Barking during the early years of the war.

"So the long hot summer went by. I learned to fire a rifle and make petrol bombs. Nowadays it seems as though all children learn these things in elementary school, but we had to teach ourselves ...

One day a demonstration was held in a field, and some high brass, including a General, came to see what we were doing. The field had a hill in it and an old car was pushed down it as a target. The whole thing was a fiasco. We found it was not so easy to hit a moving object with a sherry bottle filled with fluid, for the thing is so cumbersome. Most of us missed, and I nearly hit the General who had been unwise enough to stand opposite me. Two bottles did hit the car and they just bounced off unbroken. Obviously, we had to do some more thinking."

Barking
M.O.'S DEPARTURE
GIFTS FOR DR. COCKBURN

Members of the local A.R.P. services and friends assembled in large numbers at the Municipal Restaurant on Monday evening to bid farewell to Dr. T. A. Cockburn, who is leaving the district after two years as Assistant Medical Officer. Among the guests were representatives from all the first aid posts, the hospitals, the control room, and other civil defence departments. An enjoyable programme included dancing, parlour games and a cabaret show.

An interesting feature of the proceedings was the presentation of gifts to Dr. Cockburn on behalf of the personnel of the Central Clinic Depot. They were a stethoscope, a travelling clock, a set of hair-brushes, and an album containing the autographs of the subscribers.

Making the presentation Mrs. Hills said the gifts were a small token of their respect, esteem and appreciation of the services he had rendered A.R.P. workers in Barking. They were particularly indebted to Dr. Cockburn for the lectures he had given and which had made them efficient in their work.

DEBT OF GRATITUDE

He had an exceptionally interesting and effective method of imparting knowledge to others, and they owed him a very great debt of gratitude. Apart from the more serious aspect—he realized that all work and no play was a mistake even in these days of stress—he had organized some wonderful entertainments during the black-out and the blitz. When other people were inclined to stay indoors he had continued with the good work of providing amusement for civil defence workers and others. They were all sorry that he was going, and would miss him greatly. With their gifts went their best wishes for his future.

Dr. Cockburn, expressing thanks, said he had been very happy with them in Barking, where he had made many friends, especially since the beginning of the war. He was sorry to go, and would retain many memories of happy times spent with them. They had been a happy party at the Central Clinic, and he wished to thank them for the support they had accorded him in his efforts to provide entertainment so that they could relax. They were justly entitled to some form of pleasure to break the monotony of long duty periods. They had played in very unusual circumstances. He remembered playing cards with one of the women workers who, after failing three times with her "calls," secured a "cast-iron" hand. Just then a bomb dropped not far away, but she insisted that the game should be finished. It had been delightful to meet them at the many admirable functions that had been arranged. They had enjoyed themselves even through the blitz, and that was all to the good.

Barking ARP training at the Ministry of Home Security School, Falfield, Gloucestershire, October 1939. The photographs show an incendiary bomb being dealt with (bottom) and decontamination squads at work (top).

Ford Fire Brigade (Photograph courtesy of Corporate History Office, Ford Motor Company, Brentwood)

" ... The Fire Brigade, (consisted) of twenty fully-trained firemen always on duty in each shift, manning two fully-equipped fire engines and one trailer pump. Altogether there were sixty-nine fire guards continuously on duty by day, and fifty-five by night. They worked in conjunction with the Factory Service Staff of eighteen men a shift, trained both as emergency fire guards and fire fighters, the decontamination, rescue and demolition squads, and the first-aid parties, of which there were four in addition to a hundred first-aid men distributed throughout the shelters".

(From "Ford at war")

May & Baker Fire Brigade, 1939. First and second left on the front row are L. E. Fisher and W. T. Beeson who were awarded the George Medal in 1940. Their story is told in "A history of May & Baker, 1834-1984," by Judy Slinn. (Photograph courtesy of Rhône-Poulenc (UK) Ltd.)

A direct hit on storage hangers at May & Baker on 16th October, 1940, caused a fierce sodium fire. It was at this incident that Beeson and Fisher won their George Medals.

View from the Power House, Ford Motor Company, by Helen McKie. This picture was used in the book "Ford at War". The giant four-chimneyed Power House produced enough electricity to supply a town of 180,000 inhabitants with light and heat. The Ford Company was asked to form a Home Guard unit at Dagenham, and on 27th May, 1940, the first twenty men enrolled. A year and a half later, the unit numbered four hundred, and eventually attained a strength of some six hundred officers and men under the command of Major B. R. More.

Ford Motor Company presented over 450 mobile canteens for use in the war. (Photograph courtesy of Corporate History Office, Ford Motor Company, Brentwood).

Barking Home Guard with Hotchkiss machine gun in a pill-box. Precise date and location not known. The Battalion headquarters was in Movers Lane.

May & Baker Home Guard detachment, 1942. (Photograph courtesy of Rhône-Poulenc (UK) Ltd.

Charles Thomas Cubitt, who lived in St Margaret's Road, Barking, and served in Barking Home Guard from 18th May, 1942 until 31st December, 1944, as his certificate testifies. (Items courtesy of Mr A. G. Robery).

In the years when our Country was in mortal danger

Charles Thomas CUBITT

who served 18th May 1942 - 31st Dec. 1944

gave generously of his time and powers to make himself ready for her defence by force of arms and with his life if need be.

George R.I.

THE HOME GUARD

Home Guard landing exercises at the Ford jetty. (Reproduced with permission from "Ford works news," June 1945).

Dagenham Home Guard on parade. (Photograph courtesy of Barking and Dagenham Post).

Barking ARP, Eastbury School, 1939. (Photograph courtesy of Mr A. G. Robery). Middle front is Dick Gray, Area Warden, based at Eastbury House.

ARP (Air Raid Precautions) Wardens, taken in the grounds of Eastbury House.

CORPORATION OF BARKING

TOWN HALL, BARKING
ESSEX
RIPPLEWAY 3880

TC/T. ARP.   6th October, 1938.

Dear Sir, or Madam,

Air Raid Precautions.

I am directed by the Mayor to extend to you his grateful thanks for volunteering to serve the town in connection with the A.R.P. Scheme, and also to express his deep gratefulness for the services you rendered to the town during the period of the crisis last week.

With the easement of tension and the postponement of the operation of the Council's Scheme, the Mayor thinks that there is much to commend the suggestion that the excellent spirit and goodwill shown last week should be kept alive in perfecting the arrangements which will be necessary to maintain that good spirit, and he therefore proposes to set up an organisation (which, for want of a better name, might tentatively be styled "Barking Association of Volunteers, A.R.P. Services") to include the whole of the volunteers in the Borough, and then to divide the Association into two sections - men and women, the women to be under the Leadership of the Mayoress for the time being.

The women are particularly anxious to get started on their organisation, and for that purpose the Mayoress has asked me to invite all the women volunteers to attend a meeting to be held (under the Chairmanship of His Worship the Mayor) on Tuesday next, the 11th instant, at 8.0 p.m., at the Concert Hall, Public Baths, East Street, Barking, with a view to making arrangements for the formation of the Association and considering the terms of reference.

I am directed also to state that the Mayor will be glad to consider any suggestions made by volunteers communicated to him at the Mayor's Parlour.

Yours faithfully,

Town Clerk.

CORPORATION OF BARKING

TOWN HALL, BARKING
ESSEX
RIPPLEWAY 3880

ALDERMAN W. T. CRAIG
A.R.P. Controller

G. C. CLAYDEN
Deputy A.R.P. Controller
Chief Warden

GCC/ID.   3rd May, 1945.

Dear Sir (or Madam),

Home Security Circular No. 35/1945.
Civil Defence General Services - Disbandment
of the War Organisation.

The Ministry of Home Security have instructed me to advise you that the Civil Defence General Services are to be disbanded as from the 2nd May and from now on you will no longer be required to attend as a part-time member.

The Government have not yet made any announcement about post-war policy as regards Civil Defence, but you are invited to say whether you would wish to volunteer to become a part-time member of any post-war Civil Defence Service that it might be decided to establish later.

This is an occasion when we feel truly thankful that our task is accomplished, but at the same time, experience a sense of regret that our war-time association is drawing to its close.

I am instructed by the Council to express on behalf of the people of Barking their sincere thanks for your willing co-operation during the dark days of the past.

It will be necessary for the endorsement on the third part of your National Registration Identity Card to be cancelled, and you should make arrangements to this end at your Post or District Office.

I am also to point out that under Home Security Circular 123/44 you are entitled to retain the following items of equipment - Helmet, respirator, eyeshield, greatcoat or raincoat, battledress, boots and anklets, beret or hat, lamp, whistle. It is necessary for your signature to be obtained for any article which you retain.

I attach hereto a copy of an Order of the Day issued by the Minister of Home Security.

Yours faithfully,

A.R.P. Controller.

The official beginning and end of Air Raid Precautions in Barking. (Items loaned by Mr Wally Blanchard).

Civil Defence depot, Cambell School, c. 1939. This operated a light rescue and ambulance service. The ladies usually acted as drivers.

May & Baker ARP Wardens collecting unexploded incendiary bombs after incendiary raid on 22nd March, 1944. (Photograph courtesy of Rhône-Poulenc (UK) Ltd.

Wally Blanchard served in Barking ARP from 1938 to 1942, when he joined the Royal Navy. He was 14 years old when he joined. His father, Walter, served from 1938 to 1945, and subsequently re-joined the new Civil Defence in later years.

(Loaned by Mr. Wally Blanchard).

Ford ARP rescue service busy at work in Dagenham. (Photographs courtesy of Corporate History Office, Ford Motor Company, Brentwood).

Upon receiving information from an employee that his home had been damaged by enemy action, the Repair Squad, which was manned by a team consisting of three Works Firemen and two joiners, was immediately sent to his assistance. In all, a total of 528 houses were repaired by the Squad. When necessary, the Emergency Food Van was despatched to the scene of the incident to provide hot drinks for Ford employees and their families.

```
GB 801 b c                    London-Dagenham                     Genst. 5. Abt.   Februar 1941
(2. Ang.)                  Hauptwerk der „Ford Motor Co. Ltd."
Nur für den Dienstgebrauch  Länge (ostw. Greenw.): 0° 09' 15"  Breite: 51° 31' 00"    Karte 1 : 100 000
Bild Nr. 01121/074 (Lfl. 2)  Mißweisung: – 10° 21' (Mitte 1940)  Zielhöhe über NN 10 m    GB/E 29
Aufnahme vom 25. 10. 40              Maßstab etwa 1 : 17 500
```

TRANSLATION OF REFERENCES ON GERMAN AIR MAP OF THE
"MAIN WORKS" OF FORD MOTOR COMPANY LTD (PHOTO TAKEN 25 Oct 1940)

AREA I
1) Production & Assy Bldg.
2) Power Station
3) Workshops
4) Administrative Bldg.
5) Workers' dwellings.

AREA II
6) Production & Assy Bldg.
7) Power Station
8) Blast Furnaces
9) Coke Ovens
10) Steel Works

11) By-Products Plant
12) Gas holder abt. 50 metres dia.
13) Coal and Ore store
14) Coal loading pier
15) High line for loading.
16) Storage and Warehousing.

a) Damage

Sundry Notes: "There is a connection to the railway"   "AREA I: N-S = 500 metres; E-W = 400 metres"
"Built up area 327,000 sq.metres."   "AREA II: N-S = 1100   " ; E-W = 600   "   "
"Total extent 945,000   "   " ."

German aerial photograph taken 25th October, 1940. Note the smoke from the chimneys of Barking Power Station (bottom left) and Fords foundry (bottom right) blowing across the Thames. Anti-aircraft gun sites (Flak) have been circled. Although nearly 200 bombs fell on the Fords works and estate area, production was never seriously held up.

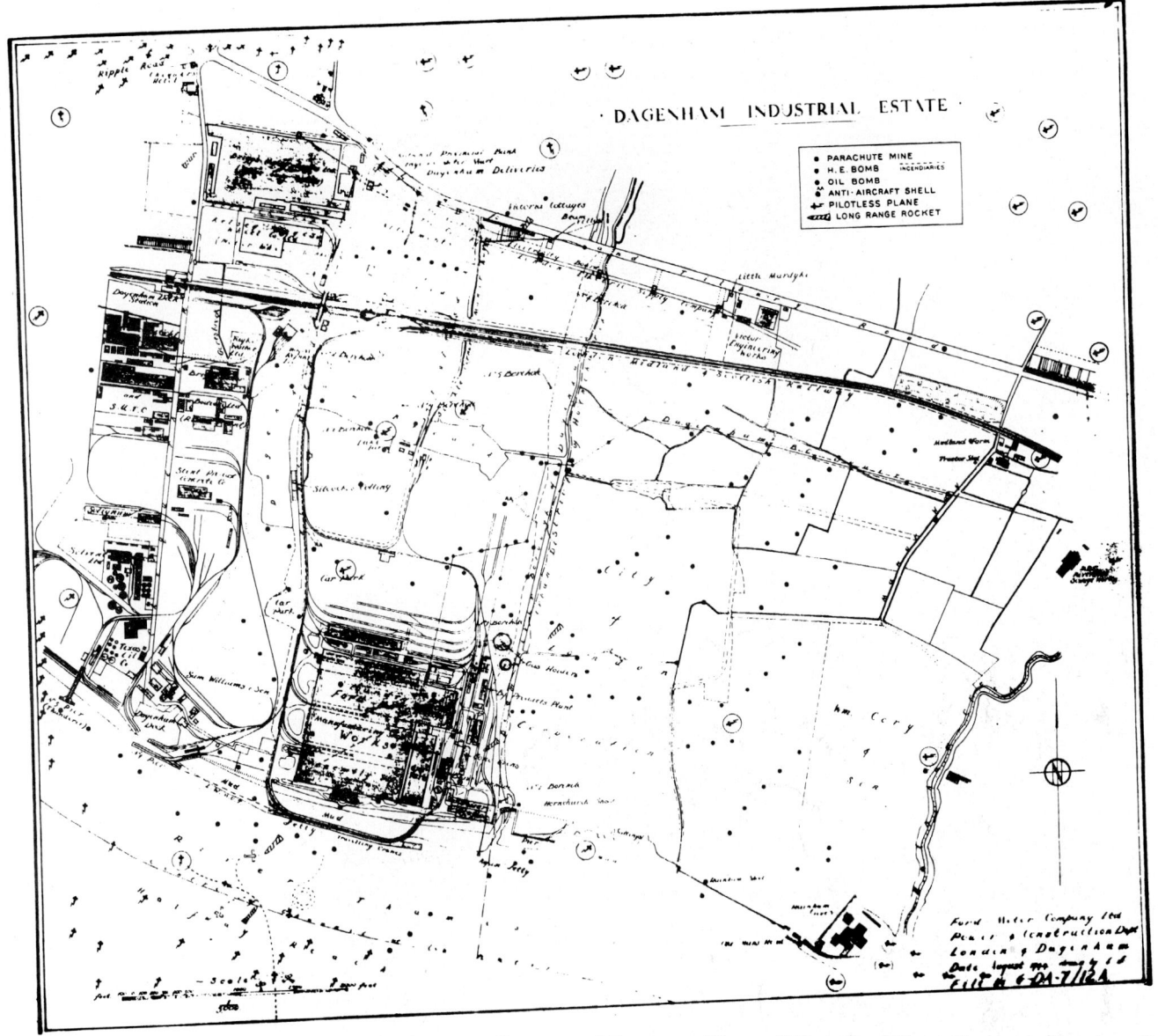

(Courtesy of Corporate History Office, Ford Motor Company, Brentwood).

The main phases of air raid attacks affecting the Borough were:

(1) armed reconnaissance attacks, from mid-June to mid-August 1940;
(2) August, 1940 until about the end of May, 1941 – the Battle of Britain and the London Blitz;
(3) the "Baedeker" raids on provincial towns, and other raids, from April, 1942, to May, 1944, when heavy use was made of incendiary bombs;
(4) the V1 flying bombs ("Doodle bugs") and the V2 rockets, which started in June, 1944, and continued until March, 1945. Many of the worst incidents, in terms of loss of life and damage to property, occurred at this stage of the War.

Incidents affecting the Fords factory area and estate.

High explosive bombs	147
Oil bombs	9
Parachute mines	10
Anti aircraft shells	9
Flying bombs (V1)	6
Long range rockets (V2)	7
Total	188

Apart from the above, a total of 79 flying bombs crashed and exploded in the vicinity of the Ford Motor Company estate.

No record was kept of incendiary bombs, which were too numerous. One night in particular is mentioned in the official record. On the night of 21st September, 1940, 284 incendiaries fell on the factory, causing about 40 outbreaks of fire.

Civic Centre – built in 1937, bombed in November, 1940! The bomb that hit the Civic Centre caused one casualty. It hit the extreme south end of the building, carrying away an overhanging canopy, and finished up somewhere in the basement.

Blitz of 1940-41

The following account was written by John J. Cook, who was born in Ilford Lane in 1925, and later lived in Linton Road and Harpour Road, Barking. From 1930 to 1939, he attended schools in Ilford and then at North Street and Gascoigne Road, Barking. The air raid in which his mother was killed occurred at Fairfield Road, Ilford. His father worked at Howard's Chemicals, Uphall Road, Ilford.

"During the blitz of 1940-41, there were many incidents that took place where I was at the time. I remember one Sunday morning, it was a lovely sunny one. After another night of bombing, I went out to buy a Sunday paper, but was stopped about half a mile from home by the police. The reason was that further up this particular road for all to see was a land mine that had been dropped during the night suspended by its parachute from telephone and power lines, swinging over the middle of the road. The swinging action was actually causing it to go up and down like a yo-yo. The area had been cleared of all people, and later that day Army Bomb Disposal drove a lorry underneath it and lowered the mine onto it and took it away and blew it up on Hackney Marshes (East London). It was funny at the time to watch this mine going like a yo-yo and there were a number of people standing watching this, might I add from a safe distance, but when I think of it now, if that ton of mine had hit the road there would have been no safe distance, just devastation.

September the 7th, 1940, was a never to be forgotten day, an all-out day-long air raid, with the whole of the London docks on fire, also many big stores and shops locally and factories all on fire. The sight was unbelievable and terrifying to everyone. In one particular incident at a Woolworth store in the area, they had a big basement, used as a storeroom. Being that this was a Saturday there were many people in the store. As the raid became worse, many of the customers and a lot of the staff went down into the basement, thinking it would be safer. But the store was hit by a number of bombs. All three floors crashed down on top of the basement; but worse was to come. The huge water mains in the High Street were destroyed by the bombs and millions of gallons of water poured down the street, flowing into shops, basements, etc. All who had gone down to shelter under Woolworths, estimated at the time around 250, were killed, mostly by drowning, it was said. Many fires this day just blazed out of control, many still burning nearly a week afterwards, all owing to the complete lack of water, so many water mains having been destroyed.

On the morning of the 9th October 1940, around 11.30am, no air raid warning had been sounded, so all of us were shattered to hear this terrible droning, which we knew to be German bombers. There must have been about fifty of them heading towards London. They had as usual followed up the line of the River Thames, but this time instead of going for the docks they had other targets in mind. In less than a minute after passing over us, we heard the terrible sounds of bombs exploding and could then see the palls of smoke rising in the not too far distance. At about the same time as the first bomb exploded, some official had decided to sound the siren.

My mother, Lily Rose Cook, age 42, used to do a favour for an old personal friend, who with old age and being crippled, could not bend down to do housework. Every week, on a Thursday, my mother used to go round and help for three hours, and she would be back home by 1pm. dinner time, when my father and myself would also be home. This particular week, for some reason, the day had been changed to Wednesday the 9th. My mother was in the old person's house and my father was at work in a big chemical factory at the bottom of this road, less than a quarter of a mile away from each other. It was the chemical plant they were after, which they did hit a number of times. My father, when this was happening, was in the factory separated by a high wall from allotments.

As the string of bombs dropped, the first one fell on the house next door to where my mother was. It completely destroyed the house and also half of the house next door. My mother was killed instantly. The second bomb of the string fell in the chemical factory allotments within feet of my father, but the wall stood still and he was uninjured except for shock."

"I arrived home for dinner just after 1 o'clock and so did my father. First obvious question was "Where's mother?" We waited a few minutes, then father said "You lay the table and I will go and see if mum is on her way". About half an hour later he came back. To my question "Where's mum?", he replied "She is in hospital seriously injured". I knew by the look of him that was wrong, and then he told me she had been killed, and followed that by saying "I have no wish to live any longer". He had his wish a few months later. He died on June 14th, 1941, of shock and a severely broken heart."

INFORMATION.

REST CENTRES
Westbury School, Ripple Road.
Church of England School, Back Lane.
Dorothy Barley School, Harrold Road.
Erkenwald School, Marlborough Road.

Secondary Centres (opened as and when required).
St. John's Church, Goresbrook Road.
St. Alban's Church, Vincent Road.
Upney Baptist Hall, Cavendish Gardens.

GAS CLEANSING STATIONS
Public—
Park Hall, Axe Street. 6, Woodward Road. Eastbury School. South East Essex Technical College, Longbridge Road.

Injured Persons only—
Broadway First Aid Post. Porters Avenue First Aid Post. Barking Hospital First Aid Post.

Vehicles—
Thames Road, River Road.

WAR DAMAGE
Office adjoining Central Hall, East Street.

SALVAGED FURNITURE
Office adjoining Central Hall, East Street.

BILLETING OFFICER
30-32, Ripple Road.

PERSONAL INJURIES (CIVILIAN) SCHEME
Claims should be made to the Public Assistance Officer at St. Margaret's Hall, Ripple Road.

IMMEDIATE AID FOR THE HOMELESS
Claims should be made to the Public Assistance Officer at St. Margaret's Hall, Ripple Road.

W.V.S.
Headquarters, Liberal Hall, Ripple Road.

EMERGENCY MORTUARY
Castle School, Ripple Road.

Secondary—
Refreshment Pavilion, Longbridge Road.

CITIZENS' ADVICE BUREAU
6A, Station Parade, East Street.

EMERGENCY FEEDING CENTRES
All British Restaurants.

From the Borough of Barking ARP guide (courtesy of Mr. Wally Blanchard).

Whalebone (formerly Beansland) House, High Road, Chadwell Heath. An early 17th century house refronted in the 18th century, it was destroyed by enemy bombing in April 1941. Photograph taken 1938-39.

Bomb damage Oval Road estate. Precise location and date unknown.

Lawrence Cottages, Marks Gate. Damaged by enemy action in November, 1940. Photograph taken November, 1948.

BOMB EXPERT SAVED RAILWAY

A RNVR officer who before the war was Deputy Director of Education for Northamptonshire, was sent for when a parachute mine landed with its tail propped against the side of a signal-box outside London Bridge Station during the raids.

If the mine had gone off, it would have disrupted railway traffic to Cannon-street, Charing Cross and London Bridge stations.

The officer, a mine disposal expert, is Lieut.-Cmdr. (then Lieut.) John Bryan Peter Miller, G.C., RNVR, of King's Cliffe, near Peterborough.

There was just room for Miller to get between the mine and the wall of the signal box to reach the fuse underneath. Three times he tried to fit a safety gag to the fuse. Twice the fuse clock started ticking. Twice it stopped again.

Then, utterly regardless of personal danger, he removed the bomb fuse, though no safety gag had been inserted. Later, it was found that the bomb fuse was leaking, so the mine had been extremely dangerous the whole time.

Lieut.-Commander Miller once made a mine safe in the muddy bottom of Roding River, which runs into Barking Creek. The mine could only be tackled at low water. Miller, with Able-Seaman Stephen John Tuckwell, G.C., reached the mine, which lay at the exit of one of London's main sewers.

Lt.-Cmdr. Miller

The bomb fuse and primer-holder were taken out. Had the clock started there would have been no chance of escape. The two men then tried to drag the mine on to a quay, but their ropes broke. Later they lifted it by a crane and made it safe.

On another occasion Miller, working single-handed, successfully dealt with a mine in a dark passage of a London warehouse.

At Coventry he had charge of a party which disabled 15 mines. It was for all these exploits that Lieut.-Commander Miller was awarded the George Cross.

35041   259

SECOND SUPPLEMENT
TO
The London Gazette
Of FRIDAY, the 10th of JANUARY, 1941

Published by Authority

Registered as a newspaper

TUESDAY, 14 JANUARY, 1941

CENTRAL CHANCERY OF THE ORDERS OF KNIGHTHOOD.

14th January, 1941.

The KING has been graciously pleased to approve the award of the GEORGE CROSS for great gallantry and undaunted devotion to duty, to:—

Probationary Temporary Sub-Lieutenant John Bryan Peter Miller, R.N.V.R.
Probationary Temporary Sub-Lieutenant William Horace Taylor, R.N.V.R.
Able Seaman Stephen John Tuckwell, P/J. 166122.
Able Seaman Ronald Lipsham, P/JX.156286.
Able Seaman Leslie Graham Parker, P/JX.178800.
Able Seaman Reginald Ernest Alfred Pearson, P/JX.131423.
Able Seaman Frank Walter Wingrove, P/J. 17269.

The KING has been graciously pleased to approve the award of the George Medal, for courage and coolness during an enemy air attack, to:—

Seaman Sam Preston Haighton, R.N.P.S., LT/JX.210778.

Sub-Lieutenant John Bryan Peter Miller and Able Seaman Stephen John Tuckwell were awarded the George Cross in January, 1941, for their gallantry in defusing a mine in Barking Creek on 23rd September, 1940, among other incidents. The dramatic story is told in Miller's "Saints and parachutes" (1951). Lieutenant Commander Duppa-Miller now lives in South Africa. He has kindly provided the following shortened version for inclusion in this book:

"Even after half a century, the adventure with that enormous German magnetic mine in the Roding River is still one of my most vivid, treasured memories.

Apart from anything else, the object was about 10 feet long and contained a ton of explosive; if used as a bomb there was nothing more devastating then in existence. Why it had not gone off was not clear. It had been dropped into the river just opposite that wharf with all those large cranes. It was quite close to a power station.

Without the instant and gallant co-operation of all concerned in the surroundings, Tuckwell and I could not even have started to tackle it. It was lying just on the edge of the central stream; but completely inaccessible. Between the stream and the wharf on the one side and the bank on the other there were yards and yards of impassable deep soft mud.

We appealed to the Borough Engineer – would there by any chance be such a thing as a canoe in a municipal park? There was. Instantly he summoned a lorry and had us driven, complete with canoe, down to a river fire station some way down towards the Thames.

Instant volunteers put us on a float and motored us up the river until we grounded some way below the mine. We paddled up the last few hundred yards ... oh joy! We found we could stand on firm chalk under the water. At grave risk to themselves several of the crane drivers insisted on standing by on the wharf in case they could be of any help, as indeed in the end they were.

Our sailors were not supposed to stand by and help us on these jobs – they should take cover some way off. We would then shout and say what we proposed to do, stage by stage. They would make a note. If the mine blew up, they could go back to the Admiralty, show their notes, and say "Next gentleman not to do so and so".

But Tuckwell pointed out that he could not possibly reach the bank before the tide had risen too far – it was already going to be necessary to work under a foot of water. I shall never forget the words which followed: "Besides, Sir", he said, "if your number is up, I should like to be with you".

We could not finish the job because the tide had risen too high. The men on the wharf let a cable down to us which we fetched in the canoe and made fast to the mine; then one of the cranes pulled it up onto the wharf, only half safe, and we were able to pull out what was still necessary".

The photograph shows the mine after it had been hoisted from the river.

Official bomb disposal record of parachute mine incidents in Barking, 23rd September, 1940 – 19th April, 1941. The first incident recorded is the mine defused by Miller and Tuckwell. (Courtesy of Barking & Dagenham Post)

The date of these photographs of parachute mine damage in Barking is given as 16th April, 1941. The control room log records several incidents for this date, including:

Ilford and Barking Joint Sewerage Works;

Paul Winn's factory, River Road (corner of factory demolished);

between Volunteer and railway bridge;

roundabout junction of Alfreds Way and Movers Lane;

Saxham Rd./Felton Rd. (2 deaths, 4 houses damaged);

marshes north of site (Power Station);

near float station;

Victor Blagdens (which resulted in oil drums falling all over the area);

on railway line between Lodge Avenue bridge and Upney Station (steam train derailed);

It was a very busy evening for the rescue services!

BROUGHT DOWN NEAR LONDON

Wreckage of the German Heinkel 111, brought down last night on Beckton Marshes, was still on fire this morning.

GERMAN AIRMAN BURIED
"SOME MOTHER'S SON"

"To some mother's son.." This was the simply written inscription on a card accompanying a bunch of chrysanthemums —the only floral tribute on the coffin of the German airman who lost his life when his Heinkel 111 crashed in flames on the marshes at Barking last week, and who was buried at Rippleside Cemetery, Barking, on Wednesday. This token was laid there by members of the R.A.F. at the request of one who wished to remain anonymous. On the breastplate of the coffin the words "unknown airman" were inscribed, the explanation being that part of the identity disc which was found on the body and was buried with it, did not include the name. Although the time of the funeral was not generally known the little cemetery chapel was almost full when the coffin, born by members of a balloon unit, was taken there for the first part of the service, which was conducted by the Rev. T. Bloomer, M.A. (vicar of Barking). Colleagues of the bearers who made all the arrangements for the funeral formed a guard of honour. The ordinary burial service form was followed, and there was no address. In one special prayer the Vicar made reference to the fact that there was "no distinction in death," and that there was "no malice or anything that would mar the soul of man towards man." The coffin was laid to rest in a grave in a new section of the cemetery, and the committal sentence was read by the Vicar. It was covered by the St. George's (Red Cross) flag.

At 12.19am. on November 19th, 1940, a Heinkel He 111 (3539) lost a complete wing after hitting a barrage balloon before plunging into waste ground on the edge of Beckton Marshes. The remains of the five crew were buried in a single grave at Rippleside Cemetery, although at the time it was reported that only one German airman had lost his life.

Several other enemy aircraft crashed in Barking, including a Messerschmitt Me 410 which was shot down by anti-aircraft on Tuesday, 13th June, 1944. The crew of two were killed, and the aircraft crashed near Choats Manor Way.

T.A. Cockburn gives the following account of the daily trials and tribulations:

"We civilians had our own little excitements, of course; a bomb blew out the windows of the clinic, a German bomber crashed about a mile away, and a Spitfire pilot parachuted into a nearby garden. But apart from this, life went on in its normal way, except that mothers who had brought their children back from evacuation areas against advice now wanted them sent back again. Scabies suddenly became epidemic and would have been quite a problem if a new quick remedy had not been found to replace the old messy treatment with sulphur ointment. But the old refrain still went on: "Eat carrots, more carrots, and still more carrots" ".

George Herbert has his own memories of the enemy raids:

"Sometimes when I went home for leaves, during the Blitz, I was glad to get back to my unit. I was in Dagenham one time when they had a terrible raid on the East End, it went on for hours and hours. The bombers were coming over in droves. The Germans were hoping to saturate us with bombs before they made any attempt to land here. Of course that was prior to them changing their mind about invading, and going to the Eastern Front. That was the biggest mistake they made, in my view – but a very welcome mistake as far as we were concerned.

This particular night, I happened to be round my brother-in-laws, in Dagenham. He'd built a beautiful shelter out in the garden, and I finished the night there. I was supposed to be home on leave seeing the missus. It was shocking, when the bombs came down. Absolutely devastating. That was the biggest raid I think of the war – when the incendiary bombs went off, it was like daylight, even from Dagenham to the East End".

This gentleman was doubtless very relieved to have been outside this shelter near the Merry Fiddlers, Becontree Heath.

T.A. Cockburn writes:

"At that time, most homes had Anderson shelters, which were folded sheets of steel half buried in the garden to form a little protective place capable of holding about eight people. They were very effective provided they did not get a direct hit."

AIR RAID SHELTERS

Anderson Shelters. A large number of Anderson Shelters have been issued and fixed and a limited supply is still available. Bunks have been issued by the Government for fixing in Anderson Shelters and a very large number have already been delivered to householders. Anderson Shelters of the small type require enlarging before bunks can be fixed and extension pieces for this purpose are available. Application should be made to the Borough Engineer. Remedial works in the form of concrete tanking have been carried out to a large number of Anderson Shelters which were subject to flooding. Householders whose shelters are unsatisfactory in this way should report the matter to the Borough Engineer.

Communal Shelters. Brick surface shelters of the communal type built in compartments to accommodate one or more families from neighbouring houses have been built in several parts of the town. These shelters are not cleaned by the public shelter maintenance staff. Cases of dampness, lack of comfort or unsatisfactory conditions generally, should be reported to the Borough Engineer.

Morrison Indoor Table Shelters. These shelters are available (subject to the necessary supplies being received) to all householders who are not in possession of an Anderson Shelter or brick surface shelter: (1) Whose occupations are compulsorily insurable under the National Health Insurance Act. Or (2) if not compulsorily insurable are mainly dependent on earnings or pensions not exceeding £350 per annum. If there are more than two children of school age in the household, this limit may be increased by £50 for each child of school age in excess of two.

In certain cases Morrison Shelters may be supplied to householders possessing Anderson Shelters or accommodation in communal shelters where the accommodation supplied is not adequate to the needs of the family. In such cases, special application should be made to the Borough Engineer. In special cases where the family is large, two Morrison Shelters may be supplied to one householder.

Morrison Indoor Table Shelters may be purchased by persons above the income limit, price £7 each. Application to purchase these shelters to be made to the Borough Engineer.

(From Dagenham's official handbook).

SEPTEMBER 1940

On September 15 we were called out to Roman Road, just off Ilford Lane, on the southern edge of our boundary with Barking. It appeared that on this Sunday lunchtime enemy bombers had swooped low over Barking, each carrying two 500lb bombs, one under each wing. It was thought at the time that the target may have been the gun battery in Barking Park or the chemical factory (Howards) in Uphall Road.

When we got there several people had cuts and other minor injuries, and of course shock. Many were taken to hospital for treatment. However, there was one terrible incident, one of the bombs had made a direct hit on an Anderson shelter situated at the end of a short garden belonging to one of the small terraced houses. A warden said that a family of six had been in the shelter, now blown to pieces with its occupants, parts of bodies were scattered over a large area, one large piece was on a slated roof. A ladies arm was brought to me, on one of the fingers was an engagement ring, we heard that the girl had been about twenty and that she was due to be married on the following Sunday.

There was a great problem here, as our Rescue vehicle only carried one shroud; and as our chaps were collecting the remains I realised that we had nothing to hold all these gruesome objects, and I sent a man to the greengrocer's shop to obtain a dozen potato sacks. Each sack was filled and labelled.

I had sent for the mortuary van, but when it arrived there was an instant outcry from local residents, they were incensed at the thought that a Council dustcart was being used, even though it had been thoroughly cleaned and painted black. We explained our difficulties to these shocked people and promised to report their feelings to the Town Hall. As a result the Council acted very quickly: they obtained a removal van from Harrison and Gibsons, a large store in Ilford. This vehicle was suitably fitted out to carry six bodies on stretchers.

To conclude about this incident, the dinner was still on the table in the back room, the family having left it to go down the garden into their shelter. The family in the next door house had survived the explosion, all suffered from shock, but their Anderson shelter had protected them from injury.

ALF TYLER, 1985

(Reproduced from Volume 1 of the Blitz then and now, published by Battle of Britain Prints International Ltd.)

IN A DOODLE-BUG RAID.

One morning we were sleeping and one of them was coming. The engine stopped, and my mother fell back into the shelter, and we covered our ears. Then it exploded and my mother ran up in her bare feet, although glass was everywhere. We couldn't get into the front room because the door was blown against it. All our ceilings were down, and the window frames blown out. When it was lighter we went to see where the bomb had fallen; two people had been killed.

Alan Dunn.

(From St. Margaret's Church of England School magazine, Christmas 1944).

Bomb damage at Fords. (Photograph courtesy of Barking and Dagenham Post).

Ford radiator and press shop interior damaged by a high explosive bomb on 16th October, 1940.

Dunkirk

"I was in Belgium in May 1940 when the Germans broke through the Maginot line, and we were ordered to destroy all stores of petrol and ammunition and to make our way to Dunkirk, where we would be taken over to Blighty by boat. Whilst crossing the barbed wire on the frontier, I got caught up in the barbed wire and could only be released by being pulled off and losing the seat of my pants. A few days later we arrived at a village where people were collecting together for the evacuation, and I walked through with a groundsheet round me like a skirt!

Getting further on we got down for the night in a wrecked house when all of a sudden shells started dropping all around us and a big oak tree about 6 feet in diameter just outside got a direct hit and all that was left was the roots in a gaping hole. We continued on badly in need of food and water and sleep, until we got to another village which was desolate and wrecked. We saw a hole beside a villa which had been an inspection pit for a garage so we just got down into this for a sleep.

All of a sudden we heard the drone of an aeroplane and it flew low over us and then came back and started to machine gun us. I was slightly wounded in the left side but we decided to get onto the road and get to our destination as best we could. By this time we were fatigued in a bad way. Eventually we got to Dunkirk which seemed to us hell. Everything was alight and bombs were dropping everywhere and our thoughts were what chance have we of ever seeing dear old England again.

But the Navy had things in hand. Men were lined up in an orderly manner, being put aboard the ships as they came in, the sick and wounded being given special attention. I know because I was one of them.

By now I was partially blind, wounded in the left side, unable to walk owing to badly blistered feet, and still minus the seat of my pants! Eventually we were put aboard an Irish steam packet and steamed for Dover. We left at about 4 o'clock in the afternoon and they told us we would arrive at Dover at about 8 o'clock but the Germans decided otherwise!

Again a new aerial attack was mounted and one of those attacks hit us midship with a bomb and another one hit us at the aft and knocked off a blade of the propellor. That put us down to half speed but with no further incidents we arrived at Dover at 12 o'clock at night where I was put aboard a hospital train for Dorset.

After several months treatment and rest I was sent to Pwllheli in Wales for convalescence and the people who took me in gave me every care and attention, waiting on me hand and foot. As a result of my injuries I was transferred to the Reserves and I went back to my job at the power station in Essex. However, that was not to be the end. I reported for firewatching with the ARP wardens and it was on one of those nights during a bad raid when we had put out a load of fire bombs and I stood outside a shelter which held about 30 people who included my mother, twin sisters, brothers, sisters in law and nephews.

At about midnight at the height of the raid I heard a terrific roar. I threw myself to the ground and from then onwards I don't remember anything until I woke up on a stretcher in hospital where I lay minus my clothes. My body was as black as charcoal. They told me they had found me at five o'clock in the morning a couple of hundred feet away from where the bomb had fallen. I was covered in debris.

But worse was to come. The shelter which my people had slept in had had a direct hit and my brother, mother and father, and brothers and sisters were badly injured. My twin sisters and brother, his wife and my nephews were missing. Where the shelter stood there was now just a huge crater.

I escaped with only a slight injury to my back and thigh. I had to keep going back and forth to the mortuary to identify the remains of my dear ones as they were found. My father is dead but my mother and sisters and brothers still bear the scars of that terrible ordeal and the graves of our dear departed ones are in the local cemetery and I still thank God for my providence."

J. W. Porter, Dagenham, Essex.

(Reprinted with permission from "We remember Dunkirk", by Frank and Joan Shaw)

"Sheepcotes", Billet Road, Marks Gate. This 16th century house, once a pub, was demolished after extensive damage by an enemy bomb in 1940.

This is a photograph of the ruins taken in 1948.

Bomb damage given as 46/48 Aldersey Gardens, Barking, September 1940.

The bomb is reported to have dropped about 10pm and went off at 3am the next morning. There was an anti-aircraft battery in Barking Park which was a target for enemy bombing raids. This accounts for many of the incidents in this area.

Bomb damage, Maxey Road, Dagenham. Precise date not known.

The Borough Engineer's Department was responsible for clearing streets of debris, repairing highways, demolishing dangerous buildings, and repairing sewers and water mains.

Bomb damage off Heathway. (Photograph courtesy of Barking and Dagenham Post)

We know these incidents occurred somewhere in the Borough, but where?

We have no records of the date or locality of these incidents.

Name	Address	Age	Date of Death
Onslow, H.	122, Chittys Lane	35	15/9/40
Reeves, W. R.	183, Eton Road, Ilford	37	18/9/40
Bailey, Ernest	2, Freshwater Road	14	19/9/40
Bailey, Mrs. Dorothy	2, Freshwater Road	38	19/9/40
Bailey, William	2, Freshwater Road	43	19/9/40
Duke, George	48, Surrey Road	7	20/9/40
Duke, David	48, Surrey Road	2	20/9/40
Hoy, Miss Kitty	7, Cartwright Road	23	21/9/40
Ellingworth, C.P.O.	362, Copner Road, Portsmouth	—	21/9/40
Ryan, Lt.-Comdr. R. H.	Gosport	—	21/9/40
Duke, Mrs. Lilian	48, Surrey Road	30	22/9/40
Lennox, Kenneth	31, Gordon Road, Chadwell Hth.	10	22/9/40
Lennox, Mr. Sidney	31, Gordon Road, Chadwell Hth.	45	22/9/40
Lennox, Mrs. Elizabeth	31, Gordon Road, Chadwell Hth.	35	22/9/40
Lennox, Ronald Victor	31, Gordon Road, Chadwell Hth.	4	23/9/40
Evans, Charles	29, Ford Road	33	23/9/40
Evans, Emma	29, Ford Road	35	23/9/40
Evans, Joyce	29, Ford Road	12	23/9/40
Evans, Raymond	29, Ford Road	9	23/9/40
Evans, Bryan	29, Ford Road	2	23/9/40
Mollenhoff, Ernest	219, Hunters Square	29	30/9/40
Mollenhoff, Ethel	219, Hunters Square	28	30/9/40
Hopkins, Rosina	145, Grafton Road	24	30/9/40
Hopkins, Harry	145, Grafton Road	26	30/9/40
Neall, James	59, Oglethorpe Road	34	2/10/40
Neall, Charlotte	59, Oglethorpe Road	33	2/10/40
Brown, Dennis	230, Halbutt Street	30	5/10/40
Brown, Moira	230, Halbutt Street	6	5/10/40
Cole, Mary	3, Halbutt Gardens	7	5/10/40
Macey, John H.	3, Halbutt Gardens	26	5/10/40
Cole, Mrs.	3, Halbutt Gardens	—	5/10/40
Cole, Thomas	3, Halbutt Gardens	12	5/10/40
Roberts, Eunice	234, Halbutt Street	—	5/10/40
Lamb, Mr.	46, Windsor Road	75	5/10/40
Lamb, Mrs.	46, Windsor Road	69	5/10/40
Mann, Mrs. Florence	232, Halbutt Street	29	5/10/40
Mann, John	232, Halbutt Street	34	5/10/40
Mann, Mrs. Elizabeth	232, Halbutt Street	34	5/10/40
Mann, Charles	232, Halbutt Street	6	5/10/40
Mann, Iris	232, Halbutt Street	4	5/10/40
Mann, Joyce	232, Halbutt Street	1	5/10/40
Mann, Mr. George	232, Halbutt Street	28	5/10/40
Mann, Mr. James	232, Halbutt Street	—	5/10/40
Mann, Mrs. Eliz. (Snr.)	232, Halbutt Street	—	5/10/40
Mann, Anne	232, Halbutt Street	32	5/10/40
Mann, Lilian	232, Halbutt Street	30	5/10/40
Martin, Elizabeth	52, Windsor Road	24	5/10/40
Martin, Henry	52, Windsor Road	35	5/10/40
Martin, Ronald	52, Windsor Road	3 mths.	5/10/40
Martin, Sylvia	52, Windsor Road	3	5/10/40
Ash, Lt. (Bcmb Dis. Sqd.)	Barracks, Gordon Fields, Ilford	—	7/10/40
Foster, Lt. (B.D.S.)	Barracks, Gordon Fields, Ilford	—	7/10/40
Lewis, Sapper	Barracks, Gordon Fields, Ilford	—	7/10/40
Websdale, Sapper	Barracks, Gordon Fields, Ilford	—	7/10/40
Hitchcock, Sapper	Barracks, Gordon Fields, Ilford	—	7/10/40

This page from "Danger over Dagenham" tells several tragic stories. On October 5th, 1940, a bomb landed in the midst of a cluster of Anderson shelters grouped at the bottom of converging gardens at the junction of Halbutt Street and Thompson Road. A total of 18 people were killed, including 11 members of the Mann family at 232, Halbutt Street. The only survivor was a very young boy evacuated to Cornwall, who was taken in by a relative from another part of London. Six people in Windsor Road were killed the same night.

Chief Petty Officer Reginald Vincent Ellingworth and Lieutenant Commander Richard H. Ryan were killed on 21st September, 1940, whilst trying to render harmless a bomb which was hanging by a parachute in a building (some accounts give "warehouse" others a "house"). The place of death is given as Oval Road North, Dagenham, and the cause of death "due to war operations". Both men received posthumous awards of the George Cross.

The last five names are those of a bomb disposal squad who were killed getting out an unexploded bomb in Connor Road.

T.A. Cockburn tells us more about the local bomb disposal squad:

"The Germans were dropping parachute mines in the Thames to sink ships. Many of them missed their marks and landed in Barking, particularly that marshy part next to the river. We had a bomb disposal squad headed by Lt. Ash, a very brave man. One day his crew was busy elsewhere, so he asked for volunteers to dismantle a mine blocking a road leading to the power station. I and a friend offered our help, so off we went up the empty road to where the mine lay, still attached to its parachute. The mine was a large globe in two parts, with flanges, and bolts through them holding the two parts together. The difficulty was unscrewing the nuts off the bolts. I held a spanner on a nut which Lt. Ash hit with a hammer. At that time the Germans had started using magnetic mines, and Lt. Ash grumbled that if the Army was going to send him on jobs like this, it should at least have given him bronze tools and not steel. It was a funny feeling looking at that mine, while he hit the spanner, and wondering what it would feel like if it went off. Would my mind register before being blown apart? And if there would be any life after death for us. Luckily, it was not a magnetic mine".

The principal hazard of magnetic mines was the fact that the clock of the bomb fuse was normally timed to explode the mine about 22 seconds after its fall. If it failed to do so, it could be re-started by the slightest movement. The amount of the clock already run off could not be known, and once it was re-started the time for escape could not be more than a few seconds.

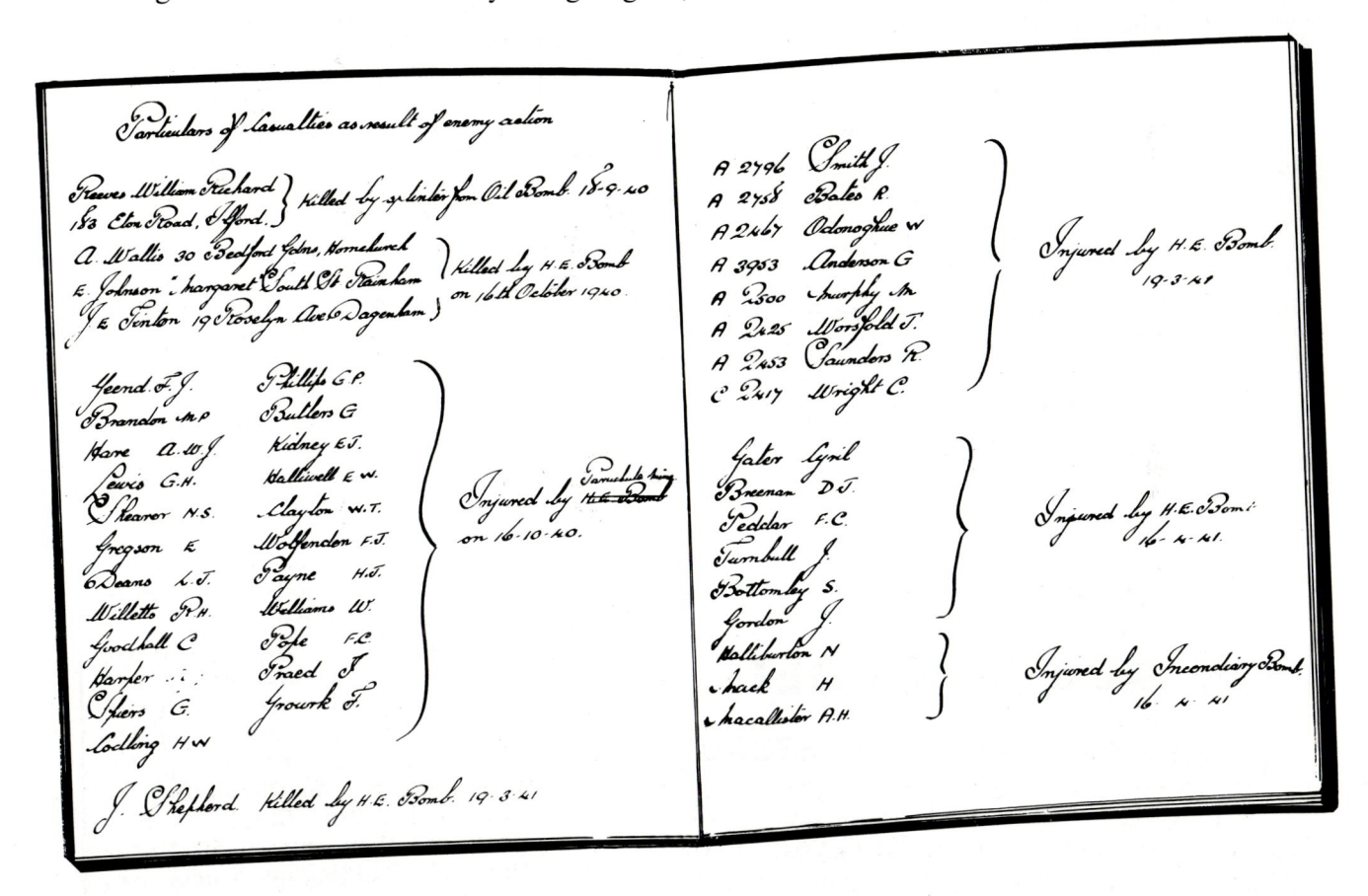

Entry in Fords Record of air raid damage & casualties. (Courtesy of Corporate History Office, Ford Motor Company, Brentwood).

Dagenham Women's Voluntary Service, outside the Civic Centre, 1940.

The first Dagenham W.V.S. centre was opened at Valence House, in August, 1940. An additional centre was arranged at 87, High Road, Chadwell Heath in October, 1942, and the following December the centre moved into new headquarters on Heathway Bridge. The W.V.S. were principally involved in staffing rest centres and mobile canteens, issuing clothing to needy cases, and helping towards the welfare and morale of the population "in a hundred and one other ways".

"The Women's Voluntary Service gave a quality of service that counted neither the time nor the place but was always there with two pairs of hands for each member clad in her green tweed coat".

PRAISE FOR THE FORCES HOUSE

DISTINGUISHED VISITORS

Recognized in high places as a model of its kind, Barking Forces House in the Vicarage Field has been inspected by many distinguished visitors. The latest was Lt.-Gen. Sir Charles Lloyd, K.C.B., D.S.O., M.C. (General Officer Commanding London District), who spent a considerable time there on Friday afternoon. Sir Charles was entertained by Col. J. Dudley Sherwood, D.L. (chairman of the Executive Committee of the Essex County War Welfare), to luncheon before going to the Forces House, where he was welcomed by Councillor (Mrs.) Martin (chairman) and Mr. W. Lungley (supervisor). He was obviously keenly interested in everything he saw, and asked many questions as to the method adopted in entertaining the troops. He expressed admiration of the garden at the entrance of the premises—the side gardens and sunk centre plot were a mass of bloom—and of the converted grandstand and additional buildings.

FINEST IN LONDON

Expressing his opinion of the establishment afterwards, he said it was a noble effort on the part of the organizers, the workers and Barking generally, and was, in fact, the finest centre of its kind, having regard to the difficulties that had been surmounted, that he had seen in London. Having heard an explanation of the transformation that had taken place, Sir Charles said he thought it was remarkable that those concerned had been able to succeed in securing such a high standard both inside and outside the building. Knowing the derelict state into which such places had been allowed to fall immediately following the outbreak of war, he was amazed at what had been accomplished, and he hoped that at least part of the fruits of their labour would remain after the war. It had been done for the welfare of the troops, who needed everything that could be achieved in that direction.

All obstacles had been overcome in a manner that was a credit to those associated with the movement. He readily supported the suggestion that an illustrated brochure should be produced dealing with the centre for circulation to other places in the country.

SCRAPING SPUDS

Sir Charles paid special attention to the catering arrangements, and interviewed the voluntary cooks and other workers, and specially complimented the cooks on their preparation of the food served. Watching one of them scraping new potatoes, he expressed the opinion that the "spuds" might be cooked in their skins, but the immediate reply was "Oh, we do everything just as we would if these servicemen and women were our own sons and daughters home on leave. Nothing's too good for them."

Another feature which impressed the visitor was that the furniture and fittings were in such excellent condition after so much use, which, he averred, was evidence that those who were guests of the house were so appreciative of the amenities afforded that they were careful not to impair them by bad treatment. He was glad that the servicemen and women were considerate in that respect, and realized that what they had enjoyed should remain available for those who followed them.

Before leaving, Gen. Loyd expressed thanks to Col. Sherwood, Councillor Mrs. Martin and Mr. Lungley, for giving him an opportunity of seeing what was being done for the welfare of the troops in the district.

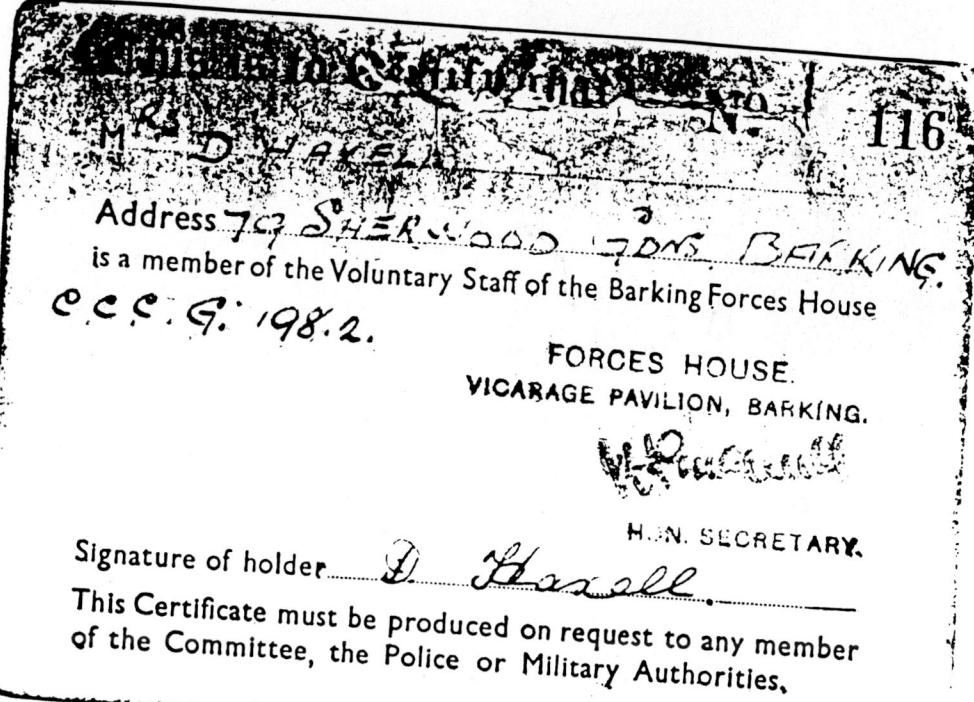

Barking Forces House in the Vicarage Field (above) was highly praised, as this cutting from the Stratford Express (25 August 1944) shows.

The Dagenham Forces House was in New Road. It was staffed entirely by voluntary labour and provided not only meals but also beds and recreation rooms. Between the date of opening in February, 1943, and July, 1945, when it closed, 14,284 soldiers slept there.

St. Chad's civic restaurant, Chadwell Heath.

Dagenham's catering service grew out of the British Restaurants of World War II. St George's (St George's Road) and Goresbrook (Goresbrook Road) opened on 10th May, 1941; Mayfair on 14th March, 1942; St Chad's (High Road, Chadwell Heath) on 22nd May, 1943; and Wantz (Oxlow Lane) on 25th September, 1943.

The British Restaurants provided cheap meals cooked on a communal basis and economising on fuel and heat. Meals were also carried in heated containers to small factories and works, and to bomb repair workers.

Originally, all meals supplied to Dagenham schoolchildren came from British Restaurants and this reached a peak about April, 1944, when 11,000 meals were supplied for the month. After this time the Essex County Council gradually established kitchens at their schools and dealt with the feeding themselves. The number of meals supplied to schools in April, 1945 had fallen to 3,000.

The following figures show the number of meals supplied and the weekly average from 1943-1946:–

	Goresbrook	Mayfair	St. Chads	St. Georges	Wantz	Total
1943/44						
Total Meals	240,161	55,324	97,744	241,262	*115,228	749,719
weekly average	4,618	1,064	1,880	4,640	4,268	16,470
1944/45						
Total Meals	169,421	40,080	88,740	156,404	130,822	585,467
weekly average	3,258	771	1,707	3,008	2,516	11,259
1945/46						
Total Meals	138,279	*23,505	76,621	142,809	108,772	489,986
weekly average	2,659	635	1,473	2,746	2,092	9,605

* Open for 8½ months only.

OPENING OF DAGENHAM'S THIRD CIVIC RESTAURANT

A WARM WELCOME FOR "THE MAYFAIR"

Dagenham's third Civic Restaurant, the Mayfair, was opened on Saturday afternoon by Mr. W. H. Kirby, London Divisional Officer of the Ministry of Food. The restaurant is situated in the Mayfair Cinema, and hot meals will be brought to it in the Ford Emergency Feeding vans which were recently presented to Dagenham by the Ford Emergency Food Vans Trust.

The Mayor of Dagenham, Alderman R. J. D. Clack, introducing Mr. Kirby, said that out of all the Ministries he had dealt with in his experience on the council, the Ministry of Food officials had always treated them the best, and had seemed the most human.

Mr. Kirby covered 96 Boroughs, which was quite an extensive job, but he tried to contact all of them personally. When he saw that a job was done to his satisfaction then everyone could be satisfied.

The committee dealing with these restaurants and other projects connected with the Ministry of Food had taken the job seriously, and they were one of the first boroughs in this part of England to start Civic Restaurants. When they started they had no one to learn from, but other places had gained from their experience. He wanted everyone to realise what a big job of work it had been.

Mr. Clayton Young, of the Ford Emergency Food Vans Trust, and Mr. Kirby, had both done much to help them with the restaurants. Although the Ford vans were intended to be used only for emergencies, the Ford Trust agreed that they could be used for places such as this.

Mr. Kirby said that there was a good reason why the Ministry of Food had gone all out to help everyone. There was one very close bond of affection between all of them, and that was the fact that we all had stomachs. That was perhaps the reason why the Ministry of Food took more interest in everyone than the other Ministries.

Not only were these restaurants a social service which had come to stay, but they were a long term policy for the future. The more restaurants we had the more secure should we feel if an invasion did... come.

It was obvious that they in London had a terrific job to do to deliver food to the thousands of retail shops who had between them six and a half million customers. If an invasion came how was it going to be possible to deliver 40,000 tons of food a week to those shops.

That was why to-day, and it was the first time he had seen it, he was so pleased to see that they were using emergency feeding equipment which, in a good many other boroughs, was still in the packing cases or out in the yards deteriorating through the weather. He congratulated them on looking ahead and getting their preparations ready.

It must have been confusing and probably a little annoying to people to read in the papers about hoarding. The Ministry of Food had just issued a statement they were scrapping the statutory order relating to hoarding.

"It is the right thing to do," said Mr. Kirby, "to look after yourselves, to keep as a reserve measure in your larders that quantity of food which you can obtain legally and food which you have produced yourselves. It is a sensible thing to keep something back from your rations every week if you can.

"The fact that you have got something in your larders is a source of confidence. If you have two weeks' supply you are relieving the strain of moving 80,000 tons of food, and you folk of Dagenham, who know something about hard work, can visualise the movement that you are saving by looking after yourselves.

"I would like to pay tribute," the speaker continued, "to the Deputy Mayor, who is Chairman of the Food Control Committee, and to Mr. Bigg, the Food Executive Officer. We have 95 food offices in London, and we can judge the efficiency and the organisation of a Food Office by the number of complaints we receive from the office and the number of complaints we have from members of the public.

"I have never received a letter from an irate housewife in Dagenham, and I have hardly ever received queries from the Dagenham Food Control Committee. They solve their problems for themselves."

During the blitz, Mr. Kirby went on, there were certain boroughs and certain large areas which were completely cut off from water, gas and electricity. The time had arrived for all of them to work out for themselves what they could do for themselves in such a situation. How could they cook their dinners. They had, of course, the Civic Restaurants and the Emergency Feeding stations.

If we all thought, "It is up to me to look after myself," one of the big things which could be done was to have field kitchens. The W.V.S., the Boy Scouts, and the Girl Guides knew all about these things. They were quite small but one could cook a good dinner on them.

Field Kitchens

He suggested that Dagenham should lead the way. If, in every ten or twenty houses there was a field kitchen, and in the case of an emergency they could cook a jolly good stew, again how much more secure they would feel.

Mr. J. Clayton Young said that some time ago Lord Perry, the head of the Ford organisation in this country, had an idea that there was a possibility of utilising a whole fleet of vans which would be ready to take food to people in an emergency. The idea was that the vans should act as the kitchens and go round to the streets where there was no water or electricity and the people would come and take the food into their homes to eat.

In the meantime, they should be used as much as possible for other purposes. In the case of Dagenham they were using them to bring food from central kitchens to outlying dining rooms, and he congratulated them on getting to work so quickly. They had very valuable equipment all over the country which could be used and should be used as much as possible.

Appreciated By Workers

Mr. Main, the President of the Dagenham Trades Council, said that the Trades Council represented many thousands of trade unionists in the district, and they welcomed the opening of such an institution as this restaurant. When the restaurant at Goresbrook was opened it was of great assistance to many workers. They hoped that before long other districts such as the Four Wantz area would also be catered for.

Alderman W. F. Legon, moving a vote of thanks to Mr. Kirby and Mr. Clayton Young, said that this was Dagenham's third Civic Restaurant, and he was sure it was not the last. The one at Wantz Corner was badly needed, and he did not want to see it delayed.

They had been using the vans ever since they had had them, and had been running hot meals from the Goresbrook Resaurant round to the factories. They were still going to be used, and were not going to be allowed to go rusty through standing about.

The vote of thanks was seconded by Councillor Bellamy.

Among those present were: Alderman Mrs. L. F. Evans, Chairman of the Food Control Committee; Alderman Mrs. Marley, Alderman B. H. Saunders, Alderman E. E. Hennem, Councillor H. L. Lyons, Councillor F. T. Grindrod, Councillor F. G. Thomas, Councillor Burridge, Councillor Butters, Councillor Mrs. Reddy, Councillor Mrs. Thomas, Mr. G. Whiting, of the Ministry of Food, and members of the Dagenham Food Control Committee.

BRITISH RESTAURANT

Another British Restaurant, Westbury, has now been established in Barking, and this, like the other two, Eastbury and Erkenwald, has already become very popular. The last available figures for a full week show that at the three municipally owned catering establishments, which excludes the old Municipal Restaurant behind the Town Hall, 5,213 dinners were served. This is in addition to 7,220 meals served under the meals for children arrangements. For that week the total number of dinners served was 12,433. Even so, the whole town is by no means covered in this respect, and there is a definite public demand in other sections for similar facilities.

So far there is no such restaurant on the south side of the L.C.C. estate, but that omission it is hoped to remedy within the next few weeks. What is to happen with regard to the Upney estate and that part of the town sometimes known as New Barking? Nothing has been done to make provision in that large area, and the only available buildings for the purpose are Faircross School in Hulse-avenue, and the new Manor Central School. Possibly consideration will be given to one or both of these buildings.

Opening of Mayfair Civic Restaurant, Whalebone Lane South, on March 14th, 1942. Situated in the Mayfair Cinema, hot meals were brought to it in Ford Emergency Vans which were presented to Dagenham by the Ford Emergency Food Vans Trust.

Similar restaurants were opened in Barking.

Ford Emergency Food Van, Becontree Estate. Dagenham was allotted two of the 450 vans which Ford Motor Company provided to the Ministry of Food. These were serviced free of cost by Reynolds Motors Ltd. They were built on the Ford 10hp chassis and contained a pie oven and a tea urn.

A mobile canteen was usually at an incident at a very early stage. Besides attending to the needs of the Civil Defence parties actually engaged, the canteen also helped to ensure that homeless persons or others affected by the explosion could be gathered together for light refreshment so that some summary could be made of the requirements of more extensive feeding later on.

By the end of the War, it was calculated that the Ford vans had carried 81,649,741 meals to docks, schools, farms and small works throughout the country.

FEEDING VANS SERVICE

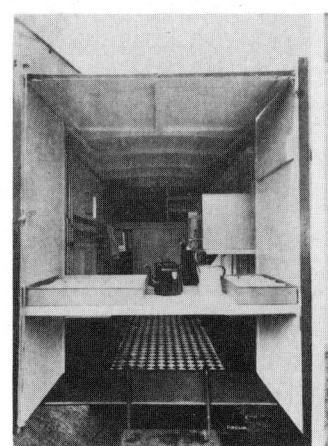

GIFT BY FORDS TO COUNCIL

A large crowd assembled outside the Town Hall on Wednesday afternoon to witness an interesting ceremony. It was the acceptance by the Mayor (Alderman W. T. Craig, J.P.) of two motor emergency food vans for use in the district from the Ford Emergency Food Vans Trust. The presentation was made by Mr. J. Stonehewer, of the Trust who was presented by Mr. J. L. W. S. Reynolds, of W. J. Reynolds (Motors) Ltd.

Mr. Reynolds explained the object of the gift—two splendidly fitted mobile units—which, he said, had been allocated to the district to assist war-time feeding arrangements.

Mr. Stonehewer said the purpose of the vans was to help to solve one of the most urgent problems affecting the civil population—to provide hot food for those who suffered as a result of air raids. Apart from that, they would be used on day-to-day work and supply food in other ways which the local officers might direct. He had particular pride in being able formally to present the vans to Barking Corporation for their use should need arise. He did so because the plan of which they were an integral part had been evolved and carried into effect by the leaders of the great industrial organization to which he had the honour to belong—that bearing the name of Ford.

The men to whom their thanks were especially due were Mr. Henry Ford, his son Mr. Edsel Ford, and Lord Perry, the chairman of Ford Motor Co. Ltd. The plan was inspired by Lord Perry. Hundreds of such vans were necessary, and the problem was solved to a large extent by the generosity of Mr. Henry Ford, who, with his son, cabled an offer to bear the cost of providing the vans, so that the plan could be put into operation with the least possible delay. The value of the gift, he was told, was in the neighbourhood of £150,000. He believed that it was the largest individual war gift made to the country by their cousins across the Atlantic. They hoped to be able to place still more vans in the service. Messrs. Kelsey Hayes Wheel Company had provided the money covering one of the vans being presented that day. He formally handed the keys of the vans to the Mayor, who inspected the vehicles.

The Mayor, who was accompanied by Alderman W. J. James, M.B.E., J.P., C.A. (chairman of the Education Committee), the Town Clerk (Mr. E. R. Farr), and the Director of Education (Mr. T. Frost), accepted the gift on behalf of the Borough with very sincere thanks. The gift, he said, would be an addition to the vans already in use in the town, and which had done such excellent service both under blitz conditions and otherwise. If they were able to accomplish half the work that was done by the old vans, they would have proved a very valuable gift.

Stratford Express.
6th March, 1942.

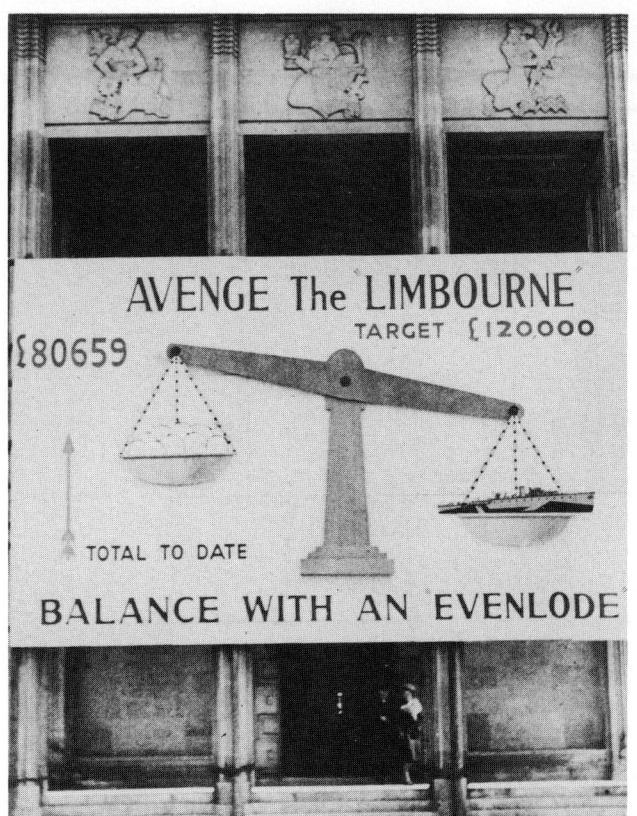

Dagenham Warships Week Exhibition, 1942.
Local Committees were invited by the National Savings Committee to raise a sum of money to provide the Navy with a ship. Those who did so were permitted by the Admiralty to adopt a vessel of the type provided. Dagenham adopted a recently launched destroyer of the Hunt class – HMS Limbourne. In October, 1943, Limbourne was sunk in action off the Channel Islands. Early in 1944, the Local Committee decided to replace Limbourne by means of an "Avenge the Limbourne" week, and eventually raised £143,000 to provide the Navy with a frigate. This resulted in the adoption of HMS Evenlode, which fortunately came through the War unharmed.

Sentry guarding Dagenham Dock, Dagenham Warships Week, January 31st-February 7th, 1942.

The "Souvenir guide to the industries of Dagenham" (1951) has the following to say about the importance of Dagenham Dock Station to the war effort:

"During the Second World War, Dagenham Dock ... played its part when the great volume of production on behalf of the war effort was being carried out by the firms there. One particularly important movement by rail was that of tens of thousands of tons of ashes to East Anglia and elsewhere for the construction of airfields for our bombing effort over Western Europe, while wheeled and tracked vehicles went away by the train load. At other times, when the use of the Thames was interfered with by enemy action, much coastwise shipping had to be diverted to rail. In one year (1943) 340,000 tons of traffic passed in or out of the station by rail".

The Evening News published the results of London Warship Week on 2nd April, 1942:

County of London	129,163,000
Middlesex	12,676,000
Essex Boroughs of Barking, Ilford, East Ham, West Ham, Leyton & Walthamstow	3,226,000
Westminster	11,500,000

London's target was 125,000,000. The final total came to 146,063,225.

THIS PLAQUE IS PRESENTED TO
H.M.S.
UNDAUNTED
TO COMMEMORATE
HER ADOPTION BY
THE PEOPLE OF THE
BOROUGH OF
BARKING

WARSHIP WEEK
MARCH 1942

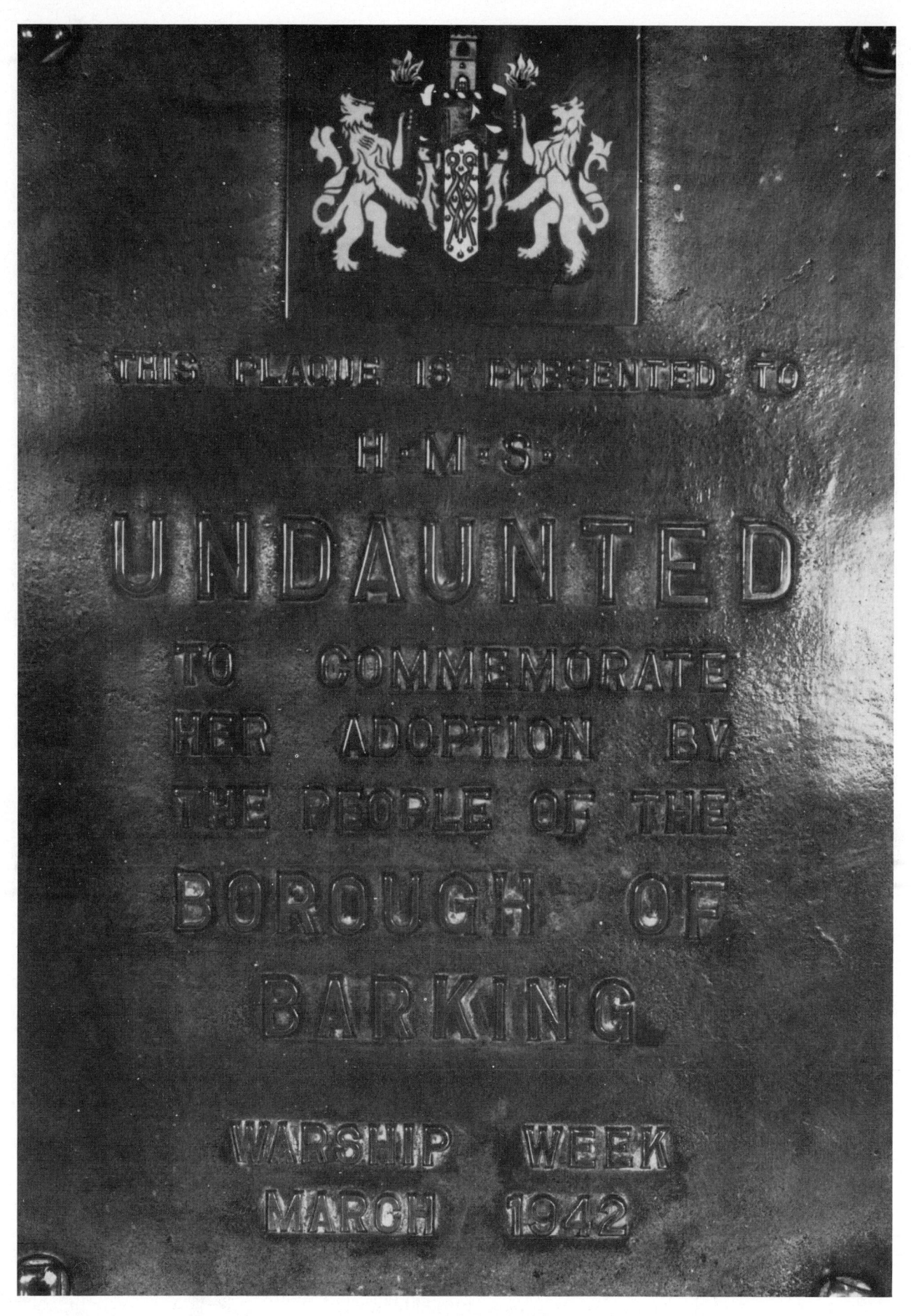

The Ulster class destroyer *Undaunted* was adopted by the Borough of Barking for Warship Week, March 1942. This replacement for the submarine *Undaunted* which was sunk on 13th May 1941 was launched on 19th July, 1943. In 1952 it was converted into an anti-submarine frigate. It is listed in *Jane's fighting ships* until 1975.

The "Dagenham" (left) and "Hudson Bank" (right) alongside No. 7 jetty, Dagenham Dock (Samuel Williams & Co.), 1955.

In November, 1941, "Dagenham" was acting as commodore ship of a convoy when she was severely damaged by a magnetic mine.

"But her master, Captain D.W. Brown, one of the finest seamen to command a Hudson (Steamship Company's) ship, managed to run her aground on Barrow Sands and there was no loss of life. The "Dagenham" was successfully salved, her cargo safely discharged and after six months she was back in service".

In the space of two years, the Hudson Steamship Company's fleet involved in the war lost ten ships. Only the "Brasted" and "Dagenham" survived. Whilst taking part in the "D Day" operations, "Dagenham" lost her master, Captain Brown, who collapsed from exhaustion and died shortly afterwards. He was awarded a posthumous British Empire Medal.

"Hudson Bank" began life as the "Empire Pioneer" and was built during the War and acquired from the Ministry of Transport.

The collection of salvage, kitchen waste and books was carried out by the normal peace-time salvage disposal plant. During the War, great salvage drives were organised in order to increase the availability of material for the war effort, particularly metals and paper. Local Dagenham school children played a considerable part in the collection of 247,220 books, amounting to nearly 47 tons, most of which were sent away to be made into paper. 26,760 volumes were despatched to the troops.

Between 1939 and 1945, the following materials were collected in Dagenham:

Metals, bottles, rags, etc.	8,315 tons
Waste paper	3,624 tons
Clinker	2,801 tons
Kitchen waste	3,336 tons
Total	18,076 tons

From Fords Works News, June 1st, 1944.

* * *

FOR THE CHILDREN

According to information received, I understand it is a fact that if all the 218 million single unit savings certificates were placed end to end they would equal a voyage round the Empire by way of Liverpool, Montreal, Vancouver, Fiji, Auckland, Sydney, Melbourne, Fremantle, Colombo, Bombay, Zanzibar, Durban, Cape Town and Southampton, a distance of 31,000 miles. This sort of news must shake the squander bug.

* * *

STAMP ON THE SQUANDER BUG

Evening Standard 18th Jan. 1943

MORE TRAMLINES FOR SCRAP

Another mile of old tramway track is being taken up from London-road by Barking Corporation. A mile of rails has already been removed from Fanshawe-avenue, and the Corporation is now considering raising all redundant metals and handing them over as scrap, making the roads good with concrete.

It is understood that while, for economic reasons, the Ministry of Works and Planning have hitherto taken no steps to reclaim these old tramlines, they are now to come under review for salvage.

The supply of scrap has up till now made a real recovery drive unnecessary.

Evening Standard 2nd Feb. 1942

Barking Cinema Aids Salvage

Similar collections were organised in Barking, with children playing their part.

Children helping to load up a special paper salvage lorry outside the Capitol Cinema at Barking, where a special matinee was given them. They bought their admission with waste paper.

The first flying bomb to fall in Essex was one at Brentwood at 11.50pm on the night of 15th June, 1944, and it was followed by one at Dagenham at 1am on the 16th June. Later that morning, a bomb fell in the grounds of Rush Green Hospital, demolishing two wards and damaging the rest of the hospital. The casualties were, 8 killed, 6 seriously injured and 7 slightly injured. Surrounding damage also necessitated accommodation of 31 persons in a rest centre. A memorial was unveiled by Aneurin Bevan (above) and the plaque, which can be seen outside Rushmead Ward, reads as follows:

IN MEMORY OF THE STAFF AND
PATIENTS OF WARD 11 WHO LOST
THEIR LIVES BY ENEMY ACTION ON
16TH JUNE 1944

STAFF NURSE ELIZABETH BARRETT
PROBATIONER NURSE JOYCE WAUGH
MRS ELSIE AUSTIN
JASMINE BEARD
981750 GNR. MICHAEL DUFF
MISS LILIAN FRY
MISS VERA HERRING
MARGARET WOOLMORE

32 flying bombs landed in Dagenham, causing 24 deaths and terrific damage. The flying bombs ("Doodle bugs") were capable of tremendous devastation. It was not uncommon to find damage to anything between 500 and 1200 buildings in closely built-up areas. The flying bomb, having cut out, generally exploded on landing, with a very shallow crater, resulting in extensive surface blast.

The effect of flying bombs in Barking can be seen in the following cuttings: Barking Advertiser.

SATURDAY, SEPTEMBER 16, 1944.

How Flying Bombs Affected Barking

Forty Three Fatal Casualties

NOW that the censorship on flying bomb news has been to a large extent lifted it is possible to give some details as to how Barking was affected. Forty-three people were killed and 460 injured, and there was damage to approximately 10,500 houses. The number of bombs which fell in the borough was 36— 21 in built-up areas and the others on marsh land or other open country.

The greatest number of fatal casualties from one bomb was eight; that was the bomb which, after striking a tree, fell on the trench shelters at Malpas-rd., near the Becontree station. Seven persons were killed in the Greenfield-rd. incident, and a similar number lost their lives at Creeksmouth. Six were killed by the bomb which fell in Mayesbrook Park, near Lodge-av., five at Tanner-st., three at Whiting-av., and three at Melford-av. Greatest damage to house property resulted from the bomb which

IN OTHER PLACES

Now turn to Page Two and read how the Flying Bombs affected other areas of Essex.

fell about seven o'clock one morning in St. Ann's-rd. Here, though about 1,500 houses over a wide area were damaged, there was not a single fatal casualty and only a few persons were slightly injured. Almost as extensive damage was caused by the bomb which landed in the grounds adjoining the education offices, and partially demolished that building. In this incident there was one fatal casualty.

The 10,500 houses, etc., involved represents about 60 per cent. of the town's total. About 4,000 of the houses were on the L.C.C. estate. Many were damaged twice and some three times. The number totally destroyed was 122 and the number seriously damaged and uninhabitable 497. Most of the schools were damaged, Dawson and Faircross very severely. The only religious building which suf-

fered was the small Roman Catholic Church near Becontree station, which was demolished. The only public house severely damaged was the Britannia—in the Tanner-st. incident—where part of the building was destroyed. The Barking Abbey School, in the borough of Ilford, was badly blasted, the chemical laboratory and gymnasium being extensively damaged.

The Mayor, Alderman Mrs. Engwell, who was on the scene of most incidents soon after the bombs had fallen, told the "Barking Advertiser" that she was impressed by the keenness and efficiency with which the various services—the several branches of the Civil Defence (wardens, ambulance, and first-aid posts), the W.V.S., N.F.S., Home Guard, the rest centre staffs, and the hospital staffs—functioned throughout. Thousands of people, Mrs. Engwell said, had had to be temporarily accommodated in the rest centres. She thought all the services were deserving of the highest praise for the manner in which they discharged their duties, which, she believed, they had done to the satisfaction of everybody concerned.

Mrs. Engwell also paid tribute to the manner in which the repair of war damage has been tackled. Before flying bombs began to fall Barking had 200 men available for this work. Now about 800 men were so engaged, the local workers having been reinforced by Ministry of Works squads, Army and R.A.F. personnel, and employees of firms from the Midlands and West Country who had volunteered to come to Barking.

The Corporation obtained some thousands of tarpaulins to cover roofs, and thus rooms have been kept dry and furniture preserved, while slates or tiles are replaced. More men will, if possible, be obtained to speed up repair work, and it is hoped to get all roofs covered before winter comes.

Comparing the flying bomb attack with the 1940-41 blitz, there is no question that in the 80 days of 'doodle-bugs' the death roll was lighter, but the damage to property was very much heavier.

OUT OF FLY-BOMB RANGE

SECOND EVACUATION IN PROGRESS

Cheerful parties of children, some with mothers, many without, parties of the aged and infirm, and expectant mothers, have been leaving these parts this week for billets in the Midlands and the North, out of range of the flying bomb.

Special trains have carried these evacuees to safety, and it is known that many have already settled down in their temporary new homes. Carefully made plans had been quickly made for this second evacuation, and registration for additional parties is taking place daily.

Details concerning the evacuation from West Ham will be found in a report of West Ham Education Committee on another page.

HAMMERS WELL RECEIVED

Reports received in West Ham from the various areas to which children have been sent, is that they are being received very well. One party leader who arrived back from Mansfield, reported that there were more people offering billets than there were children in the West Ham party.

It is stated that the children are not going as school units, but will be found accommodation in the schools in the areas to which they have been sent. It is obvious that teaching assistance will be required in the reception areas, and already inquiries are coming in from the areas on that score.

West Ham's latest figures are that there were registered for evacuation on Tuesday 135 unaccompanied children and 352 mothers and 827 accompanied children. On Wednesday there were 32 unaccompanied children and 50 mothers and 111 children, and on Thursday 188 unaccompanied children, and 136 mothers and 300 children.

4,000 FROM EAST HAM

So far, under various arrangements, there have been over 4,000 evacuations from East Ham, and the Education Office has been kept busy with inquiries. Teachers have been escorting labelled parties of children to reception areas.

The schools are being kept open, and an appeal is made to parents that unevacuated children shall attend school and not be allowed to "run the streets."

Councillor (Mrs.) E. M. Brace, chairman of the Education Committee, made a statement on the position at Tuesday's meeting of the Town Council. She said that under private arrangements since June 19th, there had been 2,312 evacuations of persons in priority classes — 796 mothers, 728 school children, 609 children under school age, 11 expectant mothers, 117 aged persons, 43 invalids, and eight blind persons. There had also been 232 unaccompanied children. Under organized evacuation to billets provided by the Government, parties totalling 1,097 had already left for reception areas, and 526 more would be leaving on Wednesday and Thursday.

"I do feel," added Mrs. Brace, "that mothers who are not going to send their children away should try as far as possible to send them to school. We are having organized lessons in the shelters, and it would be better to have these children under the care of their teachers than that they should be running about in the streets."

number of these guides remained for some days, assisting in the securing of satisfactory billets.

It is known that the Leyton parties have been distributed among the following places: Morecombe, Oldham and Egerton (Lancashire); Sale (Cheshire); Stoke, Leicester, Birmingham (Midlands); Prestatyn and Holywell (North Wales); Risca, Abercarn and Abertillery (South Wales).

The Director of Education (Mr. W. Staton, M.A.), told an "Express" representative on Wednesday that he had already received some reports of the Leyton parties, and all those reports were very good. They told of "magnificent" receptions and of quick settlings down. He thought the position was very satisfactory.

BARKING'S BIGGEST PARTY

Official evacuation from Barking commenced on Wednesday of last week, and is continuing daily.

The largest party, mothers and children under five, numbering nearly 500, left the town on Tuesday. While the schools are being used, more or less, for normal purposes, all of them, with South East Essex Technical College and Barking Abbey Secondary school and the Education Offices are open every day, including Saturdays and Sundays, for registration of those wishing to go to reception areas.

An "Express" representative who watched the assembly of mothers and children at Eastbury School on Wednesday, for the biggest exodus so far, was struck by the methodical and understanding way in which Mr. R. Galley (station marshal) and his assistants made arrangements.

CHILDREN BEHAVE WELL

Without exception the children behaved well, giving little trouble to their parents, and there were no "scenes," even when it came to saying goodbye to fathers—both Service and civilian fathers went to the school to help with the luggage, which in many cases was carried in perambulators and push-chairs.

"KINDLY RECEPTIONS"

It is now known that the Barking parties have gone into the following counties: Stafford Cheshire, Leicester and York All the reports so far received from party leaders makes it clear that the Barking evacuees have had very kindly receptions

HUSH-HUSH AT WANSTEAD

The request for information concerning the numbers an whereabouts of the evacuee from Wanstead - Woodford elicited the customary reply from the Council Offices that the authority could not give any information to the Press.

A reporter was referred to Ministry of Health official, said to have all information sought This officer gave the reply that he had not the information required.

Stratford Express.
June, 1944.

Bomb damage to Page Calnan and the Town Quay area caused by a V2 rocket. (Photographs supplied by Mr A. G. Robery)

The remains of the V2 rocket were photographed by Mr Robery in August, 1990, and the propulsion unit can be seen.

The first V2 rocket arrived in Essex at 6.35pm on 8th September, 1944, falling in a wood at Epping Upland. Three-fifths of all the rocket attacks directed against London occurred outside the metropolitan area. Barking and Dagenham received 20 rockets each.

The first V2 rocket dropped in Dagenham on Tuesday, 12th September, 1944. "It fell at breakfast time outside the Special School, Heathway, where a number of very small children were at breakfast. The building was a single storey built of wood and glass. Not one child was hurt". Luck was with the people of Dagenham more than once. On 7th March, 1945, a rocket fell behind the Eastbrook, where there was a crowded dance hall. Fortunately, no deaths occurred. The same morning one fell opposite Briggs Motor Bodies killing three pedestrians.

The worst incident in Dagenham was at Woodlands Avenue, Chadwell Heath, on January 7th, 1945. Seven people were killed, 75 injured, and tremendous damage done to houses. The last rocket in Dagenham was an air burst over the Chadwell Heath gunsite. The last missile of all was a flying bomb that landed in some gravel pits at Marks Gate on 26th March, 1945.

The anti-aircraft gunsite at Whalebone Lane North was unusual in having eight guns, most sites having only four guns. It played a considerable part in the defence of London, as did the battery in Barking Park, and is said to have been in action for 76 consecutive nights during the Blitz. (Information from *Romford Observer*, September 19th, 1990, page 10).

St. Paul's Church, Barking, erected in 1893, was destroyed by enemy action at midday on Sunday, 14th January, 1945. The Ministry of Labour premises were also extensively damaged, and there was widespread damage to houses and shops. 8 people were killed, with 52 serious injuries and 157 slight injuries. The site is now occupied by Ripple Hall, and a commemorative plaque, laid by the Marquess of Salisbury on October 22nd, 1955, is set into the wall outside.

At 9pm on the same day, 14 people were killed in an incident in London Road which most affected the Methodist Church. Marks & Spencer and the Town Hall both suffered blast damage.

BOMBED CHURCHES VISITED

BARKING'S PROCESSION OF WITNESS

There was greater significance than usual in the annual "Procession of Witness" of the combined Churches of Barking on Good Friday. Headed by clergy, ministers and surpliced choirs, a large number of churchpeople, in the course of their tour of the main thoroughfares of the old part of the town, stopped for brief but impressive services on the sites of St. Paul's Church and the Central Hall, which have been demolished by enemy action.

Those taking part were the vicar (Canon T. Bloomer, R.D.), the Rev. N. O. Porter (priest-in-charge of St. Paul's), the Revs. E. F. Hudson, J. Fleetwood and F. Erskine (curates), the Rev. W. J. Smart (Central Hall), and Pastor Stonham (Elim Church).

At the site of St. Paul's the hymn, "When I survey the wondrous Cross," was sung, and a short address given by the Rev. N. O. Porter; and at the Central Hall site the hymn, "There is a green hill," was sung, and the Rev. W. J. Smart briefly addressed those present.

Stratford Express, 6th April, 1945.

NOVEMBER 1944

BIG BEN 257

The one round the corner in Capel Gardens was most dramatic as we knew most of the people that were killed or injured. My recollection of this is that my wife and I were asleep in the middle of the night when a large flash and explosion woke us up. We were covered by broken glass and plaster, but unharmed. I dressed immediately and went round into Longbridge Road to find that the rocket had fallen in front of the centre pair of houses, there being five pairs between the ends of Capel Gardens and Sandhurst Drive; very severe damage had been caused.

Although we had a warden's post at the end of our road nobody had reported the incident to Control. I ran back to a neighbour who at that time was the only person nearby with a phone and informed Control. Almost as soon as I was back at the scene, the Barking rescue squad arrived, our Ilford chaps following soon after. I was due on duty in the morning, it just meant that I started my shift a few hours earlier than usual.

One family that we were very friendly with at the time was a Mr and Mrs Berman and their two children. Their house was right down. The daughter of about twelve was found on the grass verge, having been blown out of the house; she was not badly hurt. We soon found her parents in their bed, surrounded by debris. Mr Berman was dead and although badly cut the doctor said that his heart had failed. Mrs Berman, and her sister in another room, were seriously injured by glass; they would have been about thirty years of age.

On searching further we found the son, Harold, who had been asleep in the back bedroom; he was about fourteen. I was presented with the worst rescue problem I had experienced up to that time, in fact this was the night when my hair went grey I have always thought! The pairs of houses were well constructed with hipped roofs which had slid down in one piece into the rubble below; poor Harold was trapped under the eaves of the roof, still in bed and in such a position that any further sliding of the roof would cause him to be decapitated.

On the site at the time were a Mr Gooch and a Mr Tifield, a heavy rescue lorry driver and a light rescue leader respectively. Both of these men belonged to weight-lifting clubs, they were powerfully built and weighed about fourteen stone, although exempted from the armed forces for medical reasons. I explained the situation to them; this boy's life depended upon their strength. We had steel crowbars, six feet in length, so with Gooch on one side of the lad and Tifield on the other it was up to them to raise the roof a few inches so that packing pieces could be inserted underneath. They had not only to lift but also to prevent any further collapse which would have meant certain death for Harold. It was unusually difficult for me as I knew the boy, he was well-loved by his family, and while all this was going on he was wide awake and talking to us. Our two weight-lifters and many other men did their stuff, and we soon had Harold in hospital; we hadn't told him about his father.

Incident No.	Time	Location of Incident.	Area of Launching	Other Information
257	0540	WL904405 Between CAPEL GARDENS and LONGBRIDGE ROAD, ILFORD. (Corrected pin-point).	MONSTER Area.	Additional Information:- 5 houses demolished and 20 seriously damaged. 4 persons killed 6 seriously injured 3 trapped Radar Ranges:- Dunkirk 142.4 to 121.9 miles Time 0534 06/60 to 0534 48/60 hrs Bromley 130.3 to 126.6 miles Time 0534 00/60 to 0534 22/60 hrs Bawdsey 115.1 to 93.2 miles Time 0534 03/60 to 0534 49/60 hrs High Street 112.5 to 96.2 miles Time 0534 to 0534 44/60 hrs Based on range cuts, the Scientific Observer estimates the firing point to be within an area 2 Kms East of a line QD 5880 to QD 5884.
258	0810	Bearing of 187 degrees from ORFORDNESS in the sea.	East of The HAGUE.	Rocket trail seen by many R.O.C. Posts in Eastern and North-Eastern England. Weather at the time clear and frosty A suspected warning was given by Bawdsey II at 0803 hrs Radar Ranges:- Dover 145.7 to 141 miles Time 0801 26/60 to 0802 6/60 hrs Dunkirk 151.7 to 149.2 miles Time 0802 to 0802 9/60 hrs Bromley 141.4 to 135.9 miles Time 0801 37/60 to 0802 5/60 hrs High Street 121.2 to 116.4 miles Time 0801 40/60 to 0802 10/60 hrs Bawdsey II 125.5 to 121.4 miles Time 0801 33/60 to 0802 4/60 hrs Based on Radar Range cuts, the Scientific Observer estimates the firing point to be 2 Kms East of a line joining QD 7198 to QD 7194.
259	1101	WL967021 RAINHAM	Possibly The MONSTER Area.	Crater 30 feet by 7½ feet. 20 houses seriously damaged. 200 slightly damaged. Casualties - 2 killed 30 seriously injured 78 slightly injured Warnings were given by Bromley at 1057½ hrs, G10 at 1059½ hrs Radar Ranges:- Bromley 132.3 to 125.7 miles Time 1056 37/60 to 1056 54/60 hrs. Insufficient Radar information is available to establish a definite firing point, but the range from Bromley is consistent with the Monster Area.

This is Fighter Command's Big Ben report on rocket 257 on November 26. By now radar (augmented by sound ranging and flash spotting) was detecting rockets some 3½ minutes prior to their arrival in Britain. However, in view of the brief advance warning, no decision had yet been made over the issue of a warning of attack to the general public. In mid-November nine GL Mk II radar sets were rushed to the Continent to help complete radar cover of Brussels and Antwerp, then seen to be suffering the greater threat. Once No. 105 Mobile Air Reporting Unit became operational at Malines in Belgium in mid-December, this, in turn, helped warn London of the launch of rockets aimed at Britain. However, by the time the plots were analysed, it was reckoned that the public could, at best, be warned only 60 seconds before a rocket landed. When this was weighed up against the possible panic which might be caused, it was still believed that the better course was not to sound the Alert. What had also been taken into account was the basic unreliability of the rocket in that only one warning in six would have been followed by a hit on the UK. It was also so inaccurate a weapon that had London been alerted, only one out of 16 Alerts would have accurately predicted an incident on the Capital, a failure rate which was almost certain to lead to people ignoring the siren altogether. As a result it was felt that little benefit would be gained from sounding the Alert and this policy lasted right through the campaign. Efforts were also discontinued in mid-December to try to jam the rockets using radio signals. Initially, it was thought that the rocket might have been guided to its target by some form of radio control and jamming had been one of the first of the counter-measures adopted but examination of the remains of exploded V2s had not provided any evidence of guidance by such methods. As a result all listening and jamming stations were transferred to the Continent to support the manned bomber offensive then being stepped up against Germany.

The mortuary van took the total of six dead, one of them being a member of the RAF on leave.

ALF TYLER, 1986

We are pleased to reproduce from "The Blitz then and now: Volume 3" (published by Battle of Britain Prints International Ltd, Church House, Church Street, London E15 3JA) an account of a rocket which fell between Capel Gardens, Ilford, and Longbridge Road on November 26th, 1944.

1373 Squadron Air Training Corps, Barking, photographed in 1945.

LIGHTS UP!—NOV. 21st, 1944 (AFTER 5¼ YEARS)

    Lights went up last night,
    What a fine and lovely sight,
    All the children happy and gay
    Saying ho! ho! hip pip hurray!
    Because the lights are shining bright.
                              K. Yellop.

    The lights of Barking were so bright
    When I went round on my bike,
    But down my street was still quite dark,
    So I went round the corner for a lark.
                              G. Copeland.

    Last night the lights of Barking
    Shone brightly all around,
    The first time for a long time
    They've shone in Barking town.
    The last time that the streets were bright,
    I was just five then,
    Now the darkness turns to light,
    I have grown to ten.
                              Shirley Clarke.

(From St. Margaret's Church of England School Magazine, Christmas 1944).

LOCAL AIR CADET "V.C."

TENDED INJURED DURING RAID

The highest and most coveted honour associated with the Air Defence Cadet Corps, now merged in the Air Training Corps, the Cadet Gallantry Medal, has been awarded to 17-year-old Norman Charles Davies, who lives with his family at 54, Cecil-avenue, Barking. This has come to him with three Ilford boys—all members of the Ilford Air Defence Corps—for their gallant conduct during air raids. In further recognition of his bravery and coolness, Davies has been promoted to the rank of corporal. His splendid behaviour on two occasions in the early days of the blitz was brought to the notice of the authorities of the Corps. On the first he went among people and rendered first aid, at which he is thoroughly qualified, to a number who had sustained burns and other injuries, while incendiary bombs were falling. Meanwhile, his three colleagues were helping to deal with bombs, and, by their action, prevented fires to buildings in the vicinity. On the second occasion, Davies engaged in dangerous rescue work while high explosives were being dropped. So busy was he kept that he did not go to his home during the whole night.

Davies, who is one of very few to receive the Corps "V.C.," is employed at Pinchin, Johnson Ltd., paint and varnish manufacturers, Silvertown, with his father, but as soon as he is old enough he hopes to join the R.A.F., for which he is now training. His early school days were spent at Denmark-street School, Plaistow, and later he went to Eastbury School, Barking. A very keen sportsman, he is the holder of many medals for swimming and rowing. He has done voluntary work in the A.R.P. services at Barking.

Mr. N. C. Davies

Barking Council World War II "prefabs" in Ripple Road, before the dual carriageway was built. A photograph taken from the Ship & Shovel car park, with Castle Green estate on the far side, and the Sankey building top right.

George Herbert writes in his autobiography "A very lucky life":

"After I was demobbed, we had no house of our own. The wife had been bombed out early in 1942, and she lived alternately with our parents. So when I came home we had to live with her mother for a little while. Then after about six months the local Barking council gave us a prefab in Ripple Road. Beautiful place it was, and my wife loved it – bearing in mind that we had two children by now".

However, Barking Council were not so pleased with the "American-type" bungalows, as this cutting from the Daily Mirror of 27th February, 1946, reveals:

"We don't like U.S. prefabs," Council protests

BARKING (London) Council does not like the American-type bungalows going up in the borough—and is telling the Ministry of Health so.

"Definitely below standard," said Alderman Ted Ball to the Daily Mirror last night after the council decided to make a protest.

"In normal times our officials would refuse to accept them as fit to live in."

Notices are being put on the walls of the houses warning people not to knock in nails for fear of shocks from electric wiring.

Description by Mr. Charles Gibson, L.C.C. Housing Committee chairman, recently of temporary houses. "I think they are rotten, but they do provide cover and they have got good kitchens."

Rotary Club fancy dress ball, Eastbrook Hotel, 1944. Wilson Pritchard, Director of Solignums, is the "lady" with curly hair sitting next to the Mayor, Alderman Brown. Walter Kingsman, nurseryman, is in a top hat. Mrs L. F. Evans, MBE, JP, is bottom left. The reclining "John Bull" is Elvet Bowen.

A general view of the stage at Central Hall, Heathway, during the Ford Home Guard and ARP Service's concert in aid of Merchant Navy Charities on March 17th, 1943. The artiste performing is Mitzi Stamford. Rose Parsons is at the piano, and the Home Guard Band is seen in the background. Doris Hare acted as compère of the show. (Courtesy of Corporate History Office, Ford Motor Company, Brentwood).

Ford Motor Company Stock Department Christmas party for over 100 children of Ford men in the services, held on Saturday, January 13th, 1945. George St. Angelo, a long service employee, acted as Father Christmas. "His appearance through the Sports Club roof (added) a touch of realism which went a long way to convincing the younger children, at any rate, that there was something after all in the Santa Claus story".

A picture of Vera Lynn from the Evening Standard (29th November, 1941). Dame Vera was born in East Ham and was living in Barking when war broke out. In April, 1940, she was voted the British Expeditionary Forces Favourite Singer. Her contribution to the war effort as the "Forces Sweetheart" has become almost legendary.

Two workers snatch a meal at Fords during the war. (Pictures courtesy of Corporate History Office, Ford Motor Company, Brentwood).

A Dagenham Victory Party, 1945.

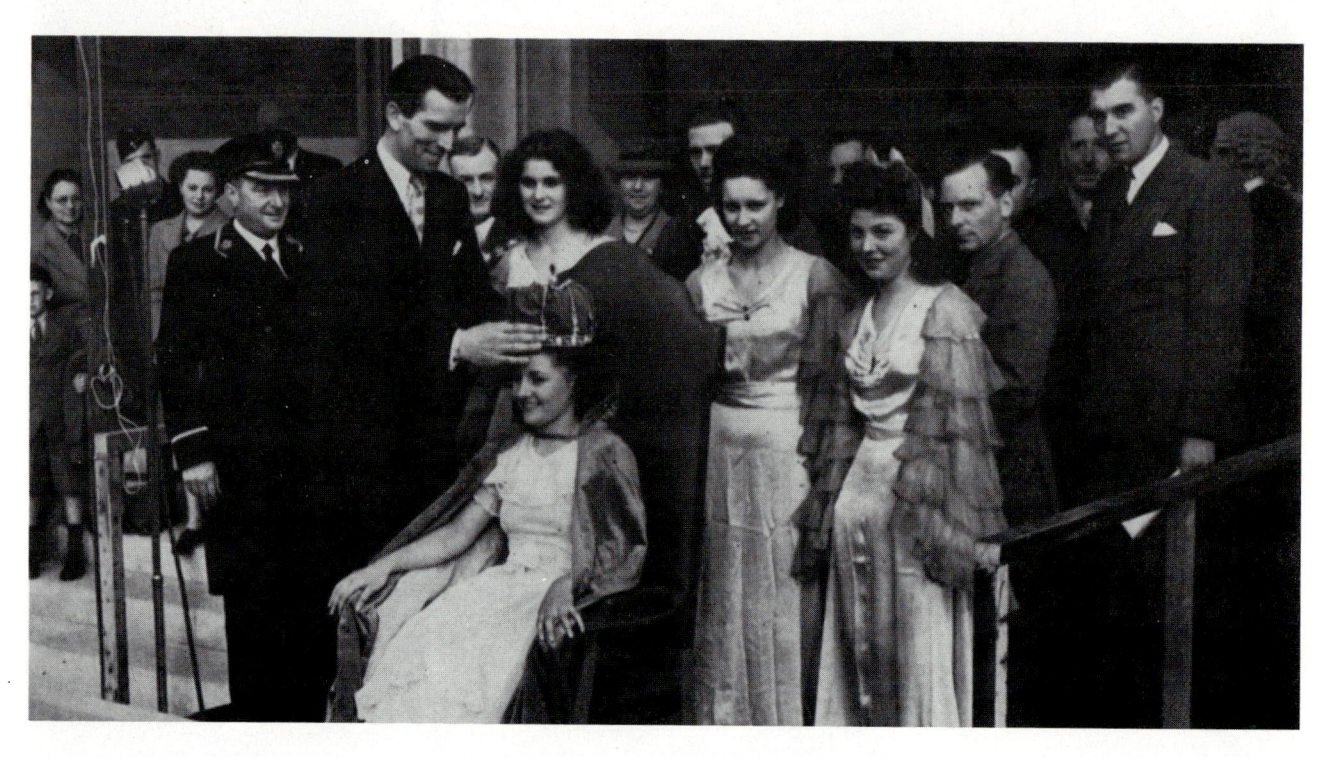

Crowning of the Victory Queen at Dagenham's Victory and Peace Day celebrations, October 6th, 1945. British film star Michael Rennie places the crown on Miss Grace Jones, with the Maids of Honour in attendance. Also present (from left to right): Mr Post (Town Hall Superintendent), The Mayor and Mayoress (Cllr and Mrs Brown), the Deputy Mayor (Cllr Thomas), and Mr F. J. Kearney (the Mayor's Secretary).

Dagenham's Victory and Peace Day, October 6th, 1945. Some of the entrants for the fancy dress competition, outside the Civic Centre.

Final party for the under fives, held at the Wantz Civic Restaurant, on November 7th, 1945, as part of Dagenham's Victory and Peace Day celebrations. Entertainment was provided by Mr Joe Barnes (at the back, his doll on the chair in the front), Mr. Treacher (at the piano), Miss Gordon and Miss Silby, Health Visitors (in fancy dress costumes), and Mr. Enever (at the back). The Mayoress (Mrs Brown) was also present.

A party for the blind held as part of Dagenham's Victory and Peace Day Celebrations, Becontree Heath, 13th October, 1945. Among those present were Mr G. Brewster, Cllr Lyons, Mr Batley, and Alderman Mrs L. F. Evans.

Party given by ARP personnel of Park Modern Depot for children who had been bombed out and taken to hospital by their ambulances. Precise date not known (1945?).

Alderman Mrs Lily Fernella May Evans, MBE, JP, delivering Christmas puddings, a gift from South Africa, to the old age pensioners in Dagenham, Christmas, 1945.

Alderman Mrs Evans was Mayor of Dagenham from 1942-44. Throughout the War she made a great personal contribution to the local war effort, despite bringing up a family of six children in addition to all her public work. As the founder and organiser of the Dagenham Forces House in New Road, she not only supervised it but lived there and cooked herself the early morning breakfast for the guests. She was head of the Dagenham Women's Voluntary Service, and centre organiser at the headquarters on Heathway Bridge. She was awarded the MBE in 1951 for her work for National Savings.

The oldest queue in Dagenham is seen here. Old age pensioners are patiently waiting for their share of the food gifts allocated to Dagenham by the people of Adelaide, South Australia. Photograph taken outside the Civic Centre, on Saturday morning, 20th July, 1946.

14,000 PENSIONERS ENTERTAINED

GIFTS FROM GOOD COMPANIONS

Nearly 1,400 old-age pensioners of 70 years and over have this week been entertained as part of the official VE celebrations and have each received a gift of 5s., provided by the Good Companions of Barking, who gave a cheque for £400 to the Mayor, Alderman A. E. Ball, for that purpose.

The first party took place on Tuesday at the Baths Hall, where the second party was held on the following day. Other parties were arranged for later in the week at Erkenwald and Cambell Schools. In each case a splendid tea was followed by the distribution of the gifts and an entertainment by dancing pupils of Miss June England, Miss Hodges (vocalist), Miss Jean Smith (accompanist) and Master Cairns, a clever pianist of 11 years. Mr. J. Gordan was M.C.

Among those who supported the Mayor and assisted in the serving on Tuesday were the Mayoress, Councillor Mrs. Ball, C.C., Councillor H. F. Savage, chairman of the Good Companions, Mr. W. T. Cockle, M.B.E., hon. treasurer, Mr. H. Coggins, social secretary, Councillor Mrs. Martin, chairman of the Old-Age Pensions Committee; Alderman A. Graham, Alderman Mrs. Engwell, Councillor W. H. Sugden, Councillor Mrs. Radford, Councillor Mrs. Beard, Mrs. Savage, and Mr. H. R. Hoad.

The Mayoress welcomed the guests, and the Mayor and Councillor Savage addressed them.

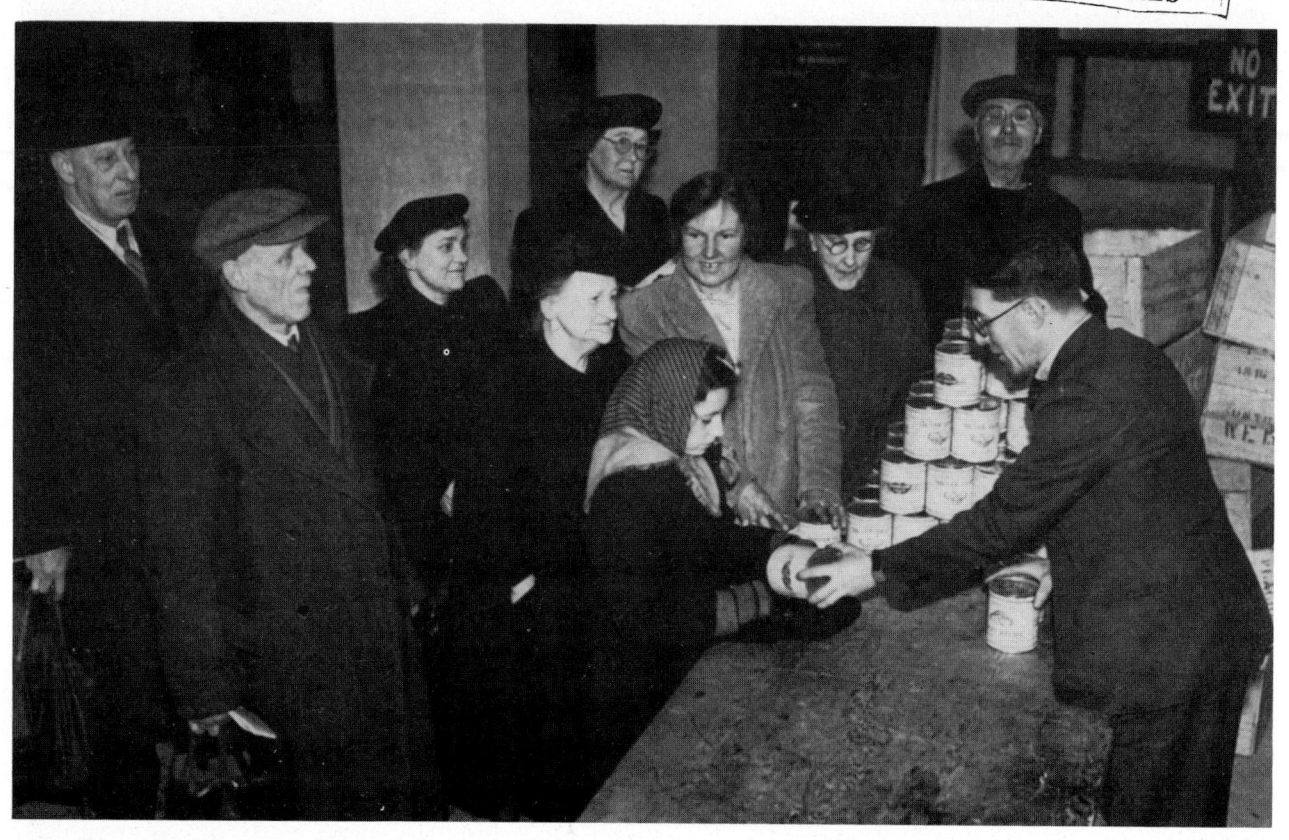

V.E. PARTIES

The Mayor, Alderman W. E. Bellamy, JP, assisted by the Mayoress, Mrs Bellamy, is seen here handing a gift of tinned pears and meat roll, plus a bar of soap, to a little girl who has come up in place of her grandmother, an old age pensioner. Photograph taken Saturday 9th February, 1947.

V-E Day on Kent Avenue. (Photograph courtesy of Corporate History Office, Ford Motor Company, Brentwood).

Life gets back to normal. Boating in Barking Park, 7th April, 1946.

DICKY BIRD, LIMITED

HIGH GRADE QUALITY ICE CREAM
and XMAS CRACKER MANUFACTURERS

ALFRED'S WAY · BARKING · ESSEX

Telephone: RIPpleway 3361-2

MANOR JOINERY WORKS Ltd.

Now fully employed on urgent war work, but ready to provide the needs of post-war development when peace returns

FLUSH DOORS · KITCHEN CABINETS
GENERAL JOINERY · TIMBER KILN DRYING

BY-PASS, BARKING

RIPpleway 3052-3-4

SWITCHES
SIGNAL LAMPS
PLUGS & SOCKETS
RESISTORS
POTENTIOMETERS
FUSE HOLDERS
COILS
LAMP HOLDERS

The Choice of Critics

Contractors to the Air Ministry, Ministry of Supply, Post Office, Admiralty, L.C.C., N.P.L., &c. Manufacturers of electrical and radio products and assemblies.

ASSEMBLIES
KNOBS
CHOKES
TRANSFORMERS
FUSES
INDUCTORS
VIBRATORS
VALVE HOLDERS

"A Complete Range"

Tel:
RIPpleway
3474
(4 lines)

BULGIN

'Grams:
BULGIN,
RIPPLEWAY
3474

A. F. BULGIN & CO., LTD., BYE-PASS ROAD, BARKING, ESSEX

WHERE MASTERS' MATCHES ARE MADE

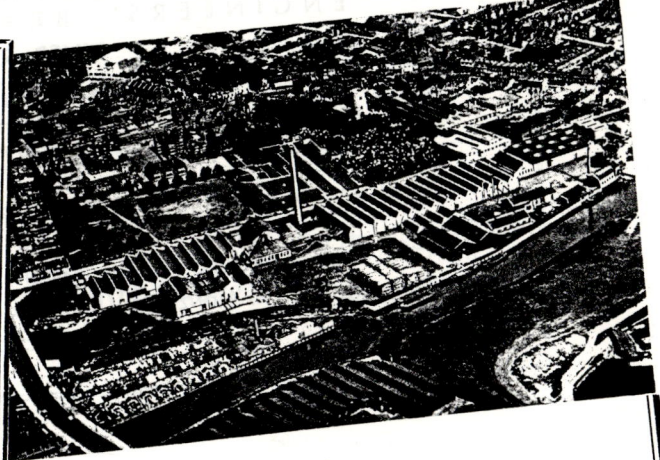

AERIAL VIEW OF
ABBEY MATCH WORKS
BARKING

J. JOHN MASTERS & CO. LTD.
HADDON HOUSE, 66a FENCHURCH STREET, LONDON, E.C. 3

For wood, iron, brick or plaster surfaces,

SHERWOODS
EST 1777
PAINTS

give you the benefit of wartime research

Sherwoods Paints Ltd, Barking, Essex

Varley DRY Accumulators

It took many years of research and practical experience to produce Motor Cars, Locomotives, Aeroplanes, etc., as we know them to-day. Similarly we worked for years on research experiment before the first DRY ACCUMULATOR was produced at Barking.

This research is still going on, playing its part in the war effort, to give to all the benefit of a

DRY ACCUMULATOR

Varley DRY Accumulators, Ltd.
BYE-PASS ROAD, BARKING

Statistics 2

CHAPTER ELEVEN

THE WORKERS' SHARE: INDUSTRIAL PRODUCTION

COMMENT and explanation on these figures of industrial production are superfluous. The men and women who did this work under skies that were at times in the possession of the enemy, were fighting their own war on a strange battlefield.

There is no Borough in England of a comparable size that can match such an output, and these are only the bulk figures. Many little workshops (and large ones) did countless small jobs.

FORD MOTOR COMPANY LIMITED
- V8 Engines 268,788
- Tracked vehicles 13,942
- Wheeled vehicles 182,511
- Tractors 120,281
- Units of electricity 810,094,794

BRIGGS MOTOR BODIES LIMITED
- Motor and armoured vehicles . . 278,000
- Store ammunition boxes . . . 8,000,000
- Jerricans (petrol) 20,000,000
- Steel helmets 11,000,000
- Aircraft components 2,600,000
- Rocket shells, bombs and components 2,500,000
- Mines, sinkers and floats . . . 150,000

MAY & BAKER LIMITED
- Cycloral sodium ampoules for Russia and Allies (anesthesia) . . . 5,000,000
- Quinacine (Nepacine) Anti-Malaria tablets . 550,000,000
- M. and B. 693 (Dagan) tablets and other sulpha drugs 700,000,000
- Menthol bromide (every plane carries fire extinguishers containing this)

KELSEY HAYES WHEEL CO., LTD.
- Wheels 2,100,000

SOUTHERN UNITED TELEPHONES, LTD.
- Yards of telephone lines . . 4,500,000,000

STERLING ENGINEERING CO., LTD.
- Lanchester sub-machine guns and magazines
- Wellington bomb release gear
- "Airborne" electric motors and hydraulic controls
- Admiralty radar equipment

Messrs. WILLIAMS, Dagenham Dock
- Bulk handling

SPRINGCOT, LIMITED
- Air frames 1,154
- Parachutes 730,000
- Sleeping bags for paratroops . . 185,000
- Gun slings 720,000
- Cotton felt . . . . . . 4,500 tons
- Palliasses 750,000

PRITCHETT & GOLD LIMITED
- Power batteries 4,850,000

W. J. BARTON LIMITED
- Loaves 50,000,000

W. J. REYNOLDS LIMITED
- Equipped vehicles 8,000
- Handling war material . . . 10,000 tons

J. CROLLIE (LUBRICATION) LIMITED
- Air sea rescue equipment

A. W. SMITH & CO., LTD. (BOLENIUM)
- Overalls for the Services . . 1,500,000

LAKESIDE IRONWORKS LIMITED
- Hot water cylinders, camp sinks and cisterns 31,000

The following statistics show the extent of Dagenham's contribution to National Savings between 1st October, 1939 and 31st December, 1945:—

Year ending 31st Mar.	Special Week	Money raised in special week £	Money raised during the year £
1939–40*	—	—	102,000
1940–41	War Weapons Week	429,000	863,000
1941–42	Warships Week	491,000	1,086,000
1942–43	—	—	780,000
1943–44	Wings for Victory Week / Avenge the "Limbourne" Week	522,000 / 143,000	1,736,000
1944–45	Salute the Soldier Week	631,000	1,883,000
1945–46†	Thanksgiving Week	642,000	1,111,000
			£7,561,000

* From 1st October, 1939.
† To 31st December, 1945.

The 10,000th tracked vehicle to be produced at Ford Motor Company during the War.

25,000th four wheel drive vehicle to be produced at Fords. (Photograph courtesy of Corporate History Office, Ford Motor Company, Brentwood).

THE FORD OUTPUT in the WAR YEARS
TRACKED VEHICLES 13942
V-8 ENGINES 268788
WHEELED VEHICLES 182511
TRACTORS 120281
UNITS OF ELECTRICITY 810094791
now for FORD CARS, TRUCKS & TRACTORS

Barton's
BAKERS
OVER
50.000.000 LOAVES IN WAR YEARS
We supplied the demands of Greater London's domestic needs. Works Canteens. Army and R.A.F. In battle and Blitz we carried on, and take this opportunity of thanking their manufacturing & distributing Staff.

SPRINGCOT LTD.
IN SPITE OF IT ALL
AIR FRAMES 1.154
PARACHUTES VARIOUS 730.000
SLEEPING BAGS FOR AIR-BORNE TROOPS 185.000
GUN SPRINGS 720.000
COTTON FELT 4.500 tons
PALLIASSES etc. 750.000

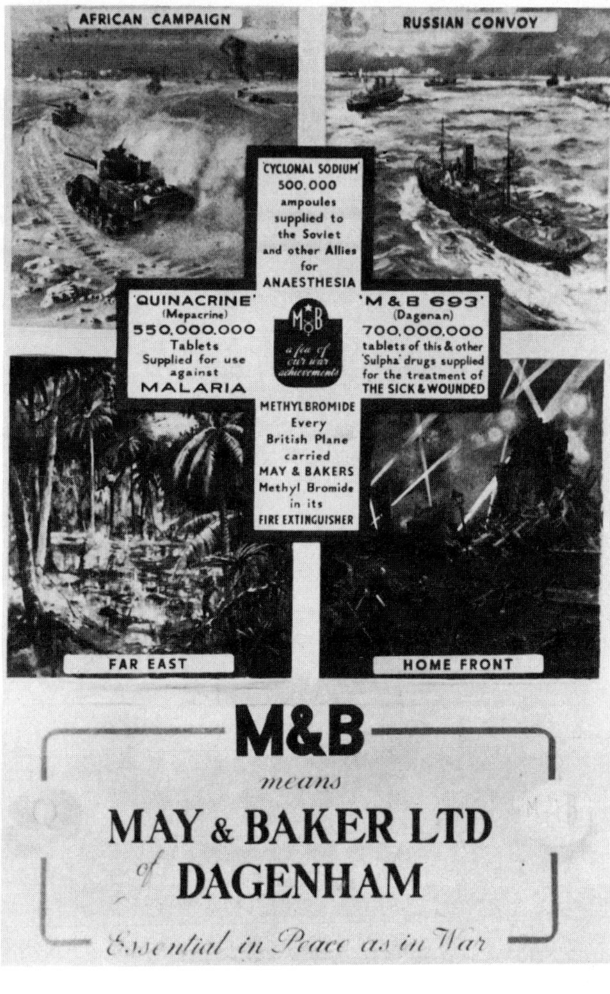
AFRICAN CAMPAIGN
RUSSIAN CONVOY
CYCLONAL SODIUM 500.000 ampoules supplied to the Soviet and other Allies for ANAESTHESIA
'QUINACRINE' (Mepacrine) 550.000.000 Tablets Supplied for use against MALARIA
M&B
a few of our war achievements
'M & B 693' (Dagenan) 700.000.000 tablets of this & other 'Sulpha' drugs supplied for the treatment of THE SICK & WOUNDED
METHYLBROMIDE Every British Plane carried MAY & BAKERS Methyl Bromide in its FIRE EXTINGUISHER
FAR EAST
HOME FRONT
M&B
means
MAY & BAKER LTD
of DAGENHAM
Essential in Peace as in War

Bibliography

BARKING, Borough Council	*Book of Remembrance, 1939-45.*
COCKBURN, T. A.	*World War II – London.* Unpublished typescript at Valence House Museum (LDVAL.2435)
COOK, J. J.	Untitled, unpublished typescript at Valence House Museum (2658/1)
DAGENHAM, Borough Council	*Air raid damage, 1940-1945.*
DAGENHAM, Borough Council	*Dagenham citizens handbook: official handbook of useful war-time information and advice.* (c.1941)
DAGENHAM, Borough Council	*Danger over Dagenham*; compiled by J. G. O'Leary. (1947)
DAGENHAM, Borough Council	*Evacuation reports of the Liaison Officer, 1939-40.* (1939-40)
DAGENHAM, Borough Council	*Home defence scheme.* (1944)
DAGENHAM WAR MEMORIAL TRUSTEES	*Book of Remembrance, 1939-45*
DEMARNE, C.	*The London Blitz: a fireman's tale.* (1980)
ESSEX COUNTY COUNCIL, Air Raid Precautions Committee	*A report ... on the organisation and administration of the civil defence services with a brief account of the operations in which they were engaged, 1939-45.* (1947)
HERBERT, G.	*A very lucky life.* (1988)
LYNN, *Dame* Vera, & *others*	*We'll meet again.* (1989)
MILLER, J.	*Saints and parachutes.* (1951)
RAMSEY, W. G., *editor*	*The Battle of Britain then and now.* (3rd ed., 1988)
RAMSEY, W. G., *editor*	*The Blitz then and now: Vols 1-3.* (1987-90)
ST. MARGARET'S CHURCH OF ENGLAND SCHOOL (Barking)	*School recorder: Christmas 1941 - Christmas 1945.*
SAMUEL WILLIAMS & SONS, *Ltd*	*A company's story in its setting: Samuel Williams & Sons Ltd, 1855-1955.* (1955)
SAUNDERS, H. St. G.	*Ford at war* (1946)
SHAW, Frank & Joan	*We remember Dunkirk.* (1990)
SLINN, Judy	*A history of May & Baker, 1834-1984.* (1984)

In addition to the above, there are many items in the archives collection at Valence House/Valence Library pertinent to the Second World War, in particular *ARP log books, War damage reports,* albums of news cuttings, and folders relating to civilian war deaths and damage to property.

"I go about the country whenever I can escape for a few hours or for a day from my duty at headquarters, and I see the damage done by the enemy attacks; but I also see side by side with the devastation and amid the ruins quiet, confident, bright and smiling eyes, beaming with a consciousness of being associated with a cause far higher and wider than any human or personal issue. I see the spirit of an unconquerable people. I see a spirit bred in freedom, nursed in a tradition which has come down to us through the centuries, and which will surely at this moment, this turning-point in the history of the world, enable us to bear our part in such a way that none of our race who come after us will have any reason to cast reproach upon their sires".

Speech given at Bristol University, April 12th, 1941, by Sir Winston Churchill.

(From: Churchill, *Sir* Winston *The Second World War: Vol 3: the Grand Alliance.* 4th ed., 1966)

HISTORY OF 1945 IN VERSE.

By a Whole Class of Poets.

When there came the last New Year
Rockets were falling far and near.
In January they fell all round about
And blew our old School windows out.
It was so cold we nearly froze
Our feet, our fingers, and each nose.
Through those dark days of noise and fear
Some nights the Doodlebugs came near.
Then dawned that day of May so bright
When the Germans ceased to fight!
Now days and nights were full of light,
And filled the children with delight.
On July 5th Elections came,
We had our School one just the same.
Before the holiday came round,
Sports were held in the playground.
The film "Henry V" in France was fighting,
In October "Macbeth" was exciting.
Shakespeare's plays are fine to see
And so for always they will be.
For Mr. Woodhouse we danced and sang,
We heard the viola and 'cello twang.
Ballet dancing by the girls was seen—
Some boys, I'm sure, wish they had been!
"Take care if you don't want to die,"
Said Sergt Robson with a sigh.
Now we reach November drear,
Hoping Christmas will soon be here,
And for 1946 a Happy New Year.

Boys and Girls of Senior 3.

(From: St. Margaret's Church of England School's SCHOOL RECORDER, Victory and Peace edition, Christmas, 1945).

Front cover: Ford Emergency Food Van attending an incident on Becontree Estate.

Back cover: Advice on saving waste materials from the "DAGENHAM CITIZENS HANDBOOK."

Cover design by Steve May of the Public Relations Unit of the Town Clerk's Department.